How to Write Great Web Content in 2020

Use the Power of LSI and Themes to Boost Website Traffic with Visitor-Grabbing, Google-Loving Web Content

By Dr. Andy Williams

https://webcontentstudio.com

https://ezseonews.com

Updated: 4th March 2020

Contents

LEGAL STUFF

Names of people, trademarks, company names, brand names & service marks are the property of their respective owners and are used in editorial commentary as permitted under constitutional law.

Andrew Williams has made his best efforts to produce a high quality & informative document. He makes no representation or warranties of any kind with regards to completeness or accuracy of the information within the book. All links are for information purposes only and are not warranted for content, accuracy or any other implied or explicit purpose. The author and publisher of this book are not in any way associated with Google.

The entire contents are ideas, thoughts & opinions expressed solely by the author after years of research into the workings of the search engines. The author and publisher shall in no event be held liable for any loss or other damages caused by the use and misuse of or inability to use any or all of the information described in this book.

By using the information in this book, you agree to do so entirely at your own risk.

The contents of this document are protected by worldwide copyright treaties and may not be reprinted, copied, redistributed, transmitted, hosted, displayed or stored electronically without express written permission of Andrew J Williams. All rights reserved World Wide.

What people are saying about previous versions of this book

"I have been buying Andy's products for a long time. I was hoping he would write this book. I am ranking on the top pages of Google for a lot of my content. I think this book is the best one he has written." **Bill Roberts**

"Forget all the mumbo-jumbo about how to outwit Google in the Search Engine ranking game with all those fancy tools etc. You might just possibly get away with some trickery and "thin" sites for a little while, but the big G will catch up with you... probably sooner rather than later. Get this book instead, read it and more importantly act on the solid (and long-term) sound advice it dishes out in spades." **Harry**

"Excellent book that is bang up to date when it comes to creating content that might actually get you ranking in the search engines. This is not theory but actual research that has led to the creation of this book." **David Sharp**

"I always look forward to anything from Andy and this hasn't disappointed." **Trevor Greenfield**

".. the first easy to read explanation I've found that shows me how to create great content pleasing both the search engines and my audience as well." **Chris Cobb**

"Well written and easy to understand. I have never been disappointed with any of the Internet info books I have bought from Dr. Andy Williams!" **J. Tanner**

How to Use This Book

This book will take you on a journey that is best followed in the order it is presented. At least for the first time. Each section builds on the previous section. Once you have been through the entire book, it then works well as a "dip in when you need it" type reference book.

A Note About UK v US English

There are some differences between UK and US English. While I try to be consistent, some errors may slip into my writing because I spend a lot of time corresponding to people in both the UK and the US. I find the lines blur.

Examples of this include spelling of words like optimise (UK) v optimize (US).

The difference I get the most complaints about is with collective nouns. Collective nouns refer to a group of individuals, e.g. Google. In the US, collective nouns are singular, so **Google IS** a company. However, in the UK, collective nouns are usually plural, so **Google ARE** a company.

There are other differences too.

I hope that if I have been inconsistent somewhere in this book, it does not detract from the value you get from it.

Typos in this Book?

Errors (and inconsistencies previously mentioned) can get through proof-readers, so if you do find any typos or grammatical errors in this book, I'd be very grateful if you could let me know using this email address:

typos@ezseonews.com

Introduction

When we think of search engines, most of us immediately think of Google. However, when I started working online, Google did not exist. We had other search engines, though, and lots of them. Here are the main ones I remember:

1. Infoseek (1995 – 2001)
2. Magellan (1995 – 2001)
3. Lycos (1994 – still going today, though it now depends on All The Web for search results).
4. WebCrawler (1994 – still going today, though it gets search results from other engines).
5. Yahoo (1994 – Still going today).
6. Excite (1995 – still going today, though Dogpile now provides its search results).
7. Altavista (1995 - bought by Yahoo in 2003).
8. HotBot (1996 – bought by Lycos in 1998). This one was re-launched in July 2011 using a robot for its mascot.

If you have been online for any length of time, I am sure a few of those will ring a bell. Some, like Yahoo, are still going today, and of course, we also have Bing as one of the top 3. However, there really has only been one winner in the search engine wars – Google.

If you could go back a few years and check out the Google search results, you'd see a very different set of search results (often called SERPs which stands for Search Engine Results Pages) to the ones we see today. In fact, even going back just a couple of years would probably show that Google has been through massive changes in the way it ranks content.

However, there is one thing that hasn't changed much with search engines like Google. They have always wanted to show the most relevant and high-quality results to their users.

In the early days of online search, the engines would typically try to match the words a user typed into the search box, with the words found embedded into the web pages in their databases.

For example, if someone typed in "Up Periscope game", then a search engine would go through the documents in the database looking for any page that contained the phrase "up periscope game". If it found one, then it could return this match to the searcher, and the search engine was happy. The search engine would be even happier if it could find several documents with that exact phrase, giving the searcher more results, more choice, and ultimately keeping them happy so they would return next time they wanted to find information.

This is where the problems began. If there were several documents, each containing the phrase "up periscope game", which one does the search engine put first, second, third, etc.?

To me, the obvious answer is to order the pages according to quality. This way the searcher would have more chance of finding a page that meets their needs quickly by clicking on the top results.

But how does a search engine determine quality?

Today, that is a closely guarded secret involving hundreds of different factors, but it wasn't always that way.

In the late 90s, there were relatively few web pages out there, and search engines just seemed happy if they could find a match for a search term. Although I am sure things were a little more complicated than that, it appeared that ranking pages was done on the basis that if a page contained a search phrase twice, it was better than a page that only contained the phrase once. Therefore, it was easy to rank a group of pages from best to worst. The page that contained the search phrase the greatest number of times won.

It almost seems unbelievable now, but back in the day, if you wanted to rank for a search phrase, you could look at the page currently in position one, count the number of times it used the search phrase, and then write your own page to contain the phrase one more time. Bingo, an instant number one ranking!

This type of "one more keyword" optimization became less effective as we moved into the 21st century, but it didn't stop the determined spammers.

As more and more websites were built, you can imagine the type of results you would see. Keyword stuffed nonsense that ranked simply because the phrase you searched for was found a lot of times on the web page. Clearly, something needed to change if search engines were going to evolve into a useful tool.

In 1998, a new kid arrived on the block:

Larry Page and Sergey Brin were two Ph.D. students and Google was their research project which began in 1996. The first version (as shown above) was hosted on a sub-domain of Stanford University.

As you can see, it started off with 25 million pages. By 2008, Google reported that its index had grown to 1 trillion pages, and then 5 years later, it stood at 30 trillion pages!

Larry and Sergey wanted to find a better way to index and rank documents. Counting the number of times a phrase was found on a page was crude and clearly didn't work. Search engine results were getting filled up with rubbish, written by webmasters trying to force their content to the top.

They introduced Page Rank. I am sure you have heard of it.

As soon as webmasters found out about Page Rank, it became the new focal point of SEO. It was the new technology to be manipulated and abused.

3

The idea behind Page Rank was probably a natural one coming from its academic environment. The basic idea was that the more important the web page, the more it would be cited by its peers.

Imagine someone searching Google for "Crohn's disease medication". If Google had 10,000 documents that matched that search phrase, instead of showing the one that used the phrase the most times in the top slot, they reasoned that the most important one would be the one that had the most links pointing to it from other web pages.

Page Rank was a kind of citation score for a web page. The more a page was linked to from other documents, the higher the score and the better it would rank for relevant search phrases.

Page Rank became the most important factor in the ranking of a web page. The more links a page had pointing at it, the higher it ranked in the SERPs. However, there was still a problem that needed to be addressed.

A web page should only rank for relevant search phrases, irrespective of its Page Rank. If someone searches for "Linux operating system", there is no point showing them a page on CNN about "cat litter", simply because the cat litter page has a high Page Rank.

Therefore, the sequence of events when someone searched for a phrase, was as follows:

1. Searcher types in a phrase.
2. Google finds all pages relevant to that phrase.
3. Google ranks the relevant pages according to Page Rank.

OK, so Page Rank was a major step forward in the ranking of pages, but Google still needed to decide which pages were the most relevant to any particular search term.

In the early days, relevance was determined to a large extent by the words on the page. A page would be determined as relevant if the search term was found on the page. Sound familiar?

In fact, the similarity doesn't stop there.

Given two pages with identical Page Rank, the page that included the search term the most times would often rank the higher of the two.

However, Google was on the lookout for unnatural looking pages. It's not natural for a web page to mention the exact same phrase 50 times in a 500-word article, is it? That would be a density of 10% for that phrase.

But what was a natural looking keyword density? Google needed to determine this, and stop any pages that lay outside of this "natural" density from ranking well.

And so, keyword density became important for webmasters.

Clearly, keyword density was not the sole measure of relevancy. However, keyword density was important enough for software to appear that could analyze the top-ranking pages on any topic, and tell you exactly what keyword densities those pages were using. By matching those keyword densities, your page would have an advantage over any other page in the niche with the same Page Rank. Keyword densities gave you a competitive advantage!

As the search engines matured, the rules for keyword densities changed.

Instead of simply needing a keyword density of let's say 5% in the document, the web page needed to include that keyword phrase in a number of different HTML tags on the web page. For example, it helped if the keyword was found in the page filename, meta keywords tag, meta description, the main page headline, the opening paragraph, several other times on the page, in ALT tags and hyperlinks, and so on.

Optimizing a web page became an exercise in trying to stuff the keyword phrase into as many HTML elements on the page as possible.

Webmasters quickly found that there was one particular place a keyword would really help you rank – the domain name.

Enter the era of exact match domains.

A search term like "buy prescription drugs online" would be really competitive and difficult to rank for, requiring a lot of Page Rank (built through inbound links). However, with this exact match loophole in Google, anyone owning a domain that contained that exact phrase would be at a huge advantage, and quickly rise to the top of the search rankings.

Exact Match Domains (EMDs) became more and more visible at the top of the Google SERPs, and many of them were spammy sites with poor content that didn't deserve to rank for those phrases.

Things like:

Buyprescriptiondrugsonline.com

.. as well:

- Buyprescriptiondrugsonline.org
- Buyprescriptiondrugsonline.net
- Buyprescriptiondrugsonline.info
- Buyprescriptiondrugsonline.co.uk

This type of exact match domain was found in the top 10 for most searches. They became a quick way to rank for just about anything, and a whole industry of buying and selling EMDs arose.

The reason this loophole existed was that the search engines, Google included, looked at the words on the page to help determine relevance to a search term. In fact, to be more specific, it was the appearance of the **exact search term** on the page that determined relevance. This was something that Google identified as a potential problem very early on. What Google wanted was a more natural way of determining what a page was about.

For example, if someone searched for "cure type 2 diabetes", Google didn't just want to return the pages that included that exact keyword phrase. It wanted to return pages that really were about "curing type 2 diabetes". Those that had the exact phrase and those that were actually about the topic were quite often not the same thing. That was because of the way webmasters forced their pages to the top using the latest and greatest Google loopholes, even if those pages did not deserve to be at the top based on merit.

What Google was trying to develop was a way to categorize a page based on all of the words and phrases on that page. Using the example above, a good quality page that should rank for the phrase "cure type 2 diabetes" would contain most, if not all of the following:

diabetes, type, blood, glucose, symptoms, complications, disease, treatment, insulin, heart, sugar, exercise, weight, risk, health, diagnosis, causes, food, test, high, medical, sign, prediabetes, eating, skin, pregnancy, doctor, gestational, eye, neuropathy, testing, diet, cells, weight loss, heart disease, gestational diabetes, high blood glucose, blood pressure, glucose testing, insulin resistance, diabetes mellitus

Why?

Because an authority on the topic would naturally use most of those words to describe how type 2 diabetes could be cured.

Most of those words are ESSENTIAL to explain how type 2 diabetes can be cured, so it follows that any page that does not use them, cannot be a quality page on the subject.

The problem for Google was that the type and amount of language analysis required to correctly identify relevant (and quality) content based on related words on a page was just too time-consuming for the technology of the day.

However, this type of theme analysis wasn't something that only appeared in the last year or two. Google has been working on this for a long time.

Back in the year 2000, Michael Campbell wrote the first white paper on themes, and then in 2003, Google bought a company called Applied Semantics which it said would help them "Understand the key themes on web pages".

In a press release announcing the acquisition of Applied Semantics, Sergey Brin stated:

"Applied Semantics is a proven innovator in semantic text processing and online advertising."

"This acquisition will enable Google to create new technologies that make online advertising more useful to users, publishers, and advertisers alike."

The press release went on to say:

> Applied Semantics' products are based on its patented CIRCA technology, which understands, organizes, and extracts knowledge from websites and information repositories in a way that mimics human thought and enables more effective information retrieval. A key application of the CIRCA technology is Applied Semantics' AdSense product that enables web publishers to understand the key themes on web pages to deliver highly relevant and targeted advertisements.

Google had acquired a technology that could help them understand web pages in a similar way to how humans understand something when they are reading it.

Using this new technology, Google went on to release Google Adsense.

Google Adsense, in case you have not heard about it, is a technology that allows Google to show advertisements on relevant web pages. With companies prepared to pay good money to advertise on the web, Google needed to make sure this technology could do more than just find a keyword on a page to confirm relevancy. Google needed to look for keyword "themes" that matched each advertisement.

Applied Semantics was the turning point for Google. It allowed Google to accurately determine the theme of a web page so that relevant adverts could be shown on that page. Google took the next logical step – incorporating this technology into the search engine ranking algorithm.

Now, instead of relying on the appearance of the exact search phrase, Google could look for themes appearing on a page to help determine its relevance to a search term.

Today, having the exact search term on your web page means very little. In fact, I want you to do a little experiment yourself. Go over to Google and search for a three or four-word phrase that has some commercial intent (in other words, a phrase someone might type in if they wanted to buy something). This is a good test because these are the phrases webmasters are trying to rank for.

E.g. Search for **buy prom dress online**.

How many of the top 10 results use the exact search term (buy prom dress online) in their title or description? How many actually have that phrase on the web page itself?

I just did the search.

I have Google set up to show me 100 results at a time, so I have the top 100 pages that rank for that term on my screen. By pressing F3 in my Chrome web browser, I can search for that phrase on the page to see how many times **buy prom dress online** appears in this list of top 100 web page titles and descriptions:

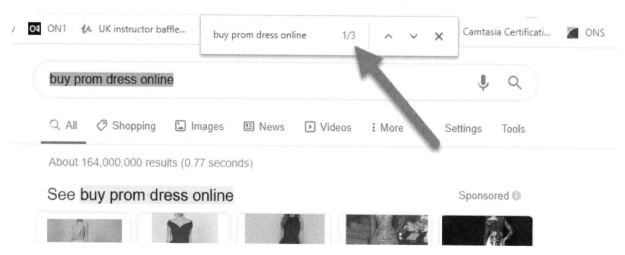

The search box says 3 times, but in fact, not a single web page listing has that exact phrase.

The 3 times this phrase appears in the search results are:

1 & 2 - The search term I typed in and a rich snippet at the top of the page:

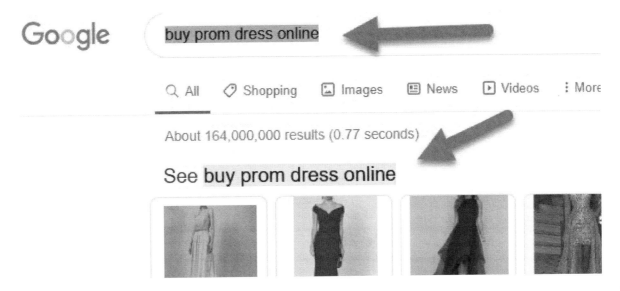

3 - The related searches section at the end, also added by Google:

So, if Google didn't rank these pages because they contain the exact phrase "buy prom dress online", why did it rank them so highly?

The answer is because these pages were themed in such a way that Google knew they were about buying a prom dress online. These pages contain words and phrases like:

prom, dresses, shop, style, dress, shipping, new, designer, accessories, long, short, lace, online, party, shoes, evening, color, black, white, low, styles, perfect, high, prom dresses, plus size, sherri hill, la femme, two-piece, special occasion, ellie wilde, faviana, rachel allan, mori lee

Whatever YOU search for in this experiment, you are likely to find the exact search phrase in some pages. However, as you can see, it is no longer essential to help a page rank well, and if you use the exact phrase too many times, it is more likely to get your page penalized.

NOTE: If you do this experiment yourself, don't forget to subtract one for the search term at the top of the results page (which you typed in), and any "Related" search ideas that Google offer at the end of the search results.

Clearly, the old method of optimizing a web page around a keyword phrase no longer works. Therefore, if you are still taking SEO advice from the "keyword phrase & density" gurus, isn't it time you changed your approach to writing content?

Let me show you a better way.

The whole purpose of this book is to give you a plan for writing content that stands a better chance of not only ranking in Google but staying there.

Before we start looking at how to write content, it's important to know a brief history of the Google algorithm changes. Not only will this help you understand where Google has come from, and where it is headed, but it will reinforce the idea that loopholes get closed, so don't waste time trying to beat the system.

A History of Google Updates

As webmasters and content writers, it is important to follow along with what Google is doing, because it never stands still. Webmasters are always trying to find loopholes, and Google is always trying to plug them.

In this section, I want to tell you about some of the major updates Google has gone through and explain why they were necessary. I'll focus mainly on those updates that affect content creators.

I should state here that we don't know with 100% certainty what many of the updates actually did in terms of algorithm changes. What I am listing here is the accepted version of events deduced by webmasters and SEOs around the globe.

Please be aware that Google releases hundreds of updates every year, so it is beyond the scope of this chapter to even try to list them all. For example, in September 2011, Google CEO Eric Schmidt said that Google had tested over 13,000 possible updates in 2010, and approved 516 of those updates.

Every Google update focuses on a specific area of the Google algorithm, but they all have one thing in common – they are designed to give searchers better results. It is that one commonality that you need to keep in mind. Going forward, it will guide you in the decisions you make about your own content.

We could go back to the very beginning to see all the changes and updates that Google has made, but I want to focus on those changes that have had the biggest effect on the way we do SEO today. I think it is important that you know this history as it helps you make decisions on which SEO strategies to avoid. So let's start back in 2011.

Changes in 2011

This was a huge year in SEO terms, shocking many webmasters. In fact, 2011 was the year that wiped out a lot of online businesses. Most deserved to go, but quite a few innocent victims got caught in the carnage, never to recover.

At the beginning of the year, Google hit scraper sites (sites that used bots to steal and post content from other sites). This was all about trying to attribute ownership of content back to the original owner and thus penalize the thieves.

On February 23, the Panda update launched in the USA. Panda (also called "Farmer") was essentially targeting low-quality content and link farms. Link farms were basically collections of low-quality blogs that were set up to link out to other sites. The term "thin content" became popular during this time; describing pages that really didn't say much and were there purely to host adverts. Panda was all about squashing thin content, and a lot of sites took a hit too.

In March of the same year, Google introduced the +1 button. This was probably expected bearing in mind that Google had confirmed it used social signals in its ranking algorithm. What better signals to monitor than its own?

In April 2011, Panda 2.0 was unleashed, expanding its reach to all countries of the world, though still just targeting pages in English. Even more signals were included in Panda 2.0. Maybe even user feedback via the Google Chrome web browser. Here users had the option to "block" pages in the SERPs that they didn't like.

As if these two Panda releases weren't enough, Google went on to release Panda 2.1, 2.2, 2.3, 2.4, 2.5, and 3.1, all in 2011. Note that Panda 3.0 is missing. There was an update between 2.5 and 3.1, but it is commonly referred to as the Panda "Flux". Each new update built on the previous, helping to eliminate still more low-quality content from the SERPs. With each new release of Panda, webmasters worried, panicked, and complained on forums and social media. A lot of websites were penalized, though not all deserved to be; unavoidable "collateral damage" Google casually called it.

In June 2011, we saw the birth of Google's first social network project, Google Plus.

Another change that angered webmasters was "query encryption", introduced in October 2011. Google said it was doing this for privacy reasons, but webmasters were suspicious of its motives. Prior to this query encryption, whenever someone searched for something on Google, the search term they typed in was passed on to the site they clicked through to. That meant webmasters could see what search terms visitors were typing to find their pages using any web traffic analysis tool. Query encryption changed all of this. Anyone who was logged into their Google account at the time they performed a search from Google would have their search query encrypted. This prevented their search terms from being passed over to the websites they visited. The result of this was that webmasters increasingly had no idea which terms people were using to find their site.

In November 2011, there was a freshness update. This was to supposedly reward websites that provided time-sensitive information (like news sites), whenever visitors searched for time-sensitive news and events.

As you can see, there was a lot going on in 2011, but it didn't stop here.

Changes in 2012

Again, 2012 was a massive year for SEOs and webmasters. There was a huge number of prominent changes, starting with one called "Search + Your World" in January. This was an aggressive measure by Google to integrate its Google+ social data and user profiles into the SERPs.

Over the year, Google released more than a dozen Panda updates, all aimed at reducing low-quality pages from appearing in the SERPs.

In January 2012, Google announced a page layout algorithm change. This aimed at penalizing pages with too many ads, very little value, or both, positioned above the fold. The term "above the fold" refers to the visible portion of a web page when a visitor first lands on it. In other words, whatever you can see without the need to scroll down is above the fold. Some SEOs referred to this page layout algorithm change as the "Top Heavy" update.

In February, Google announced another 17 changes to its algorithm, including spell-checking, which is of interest to us. Later in the same month, Google announced another 40 changes. In March, there were 50 more modifications announced, including one that made changes to anchor text "scoring".

Google certainly wasn't resting on its laurels. On April 24, the Penguin update was unleashed. This was widely expected, and webmasters assumed it was going to be an over-optimization penalty. Google initially called it a "Webspam Update", but it was soon named "Penguin". This update checked for a wide variety of spam techniques, including keyword stuffing. It also analyzed the anchor text used in external links pointing to websites.

In April, yet another set of updates were announced, 52 this time.

In May, Google started rolling out "Knowledge Graph". looking was a huge step towards semantic search (the technology Google uses to better understand the context of search terms). We also saw Penguin 1.1 during this month and another 39 announced changes. One of these new changes included better link scheme detection. Link scheme detection helped identify websites that had built their own links to gain better rankings.

In July, Google sent out "unnatural link warnings" via Google Search Console, to any site where it had detected a large number of "unnatural" links. To avoid a penalty, Google gave webmasters the opportunity to remove the "unnatural" links.

Think of unnatural links as any link the webmaster controls, and ones they probably created themselves or asked others to create for them. These would include links on blog networks and other low-quality websites. Inbound links such as these typically used a high percentage of specific keyword phrases in their anchor text. Google wanted webmasters to be responsible for the links that pointed to their sites. Webmasters who had created their own sneaky link campaigns were able to do something about it. However, if other sites were linking to their pages with poor quality links, then Google expected webmasters to contact the site owners and request removal of the bad link(s).

If you have ever tried to contact a webmaster to ask for a link to be removed, you'll know that it can be an impossible task. For many webmasters, this was an impractical undertaking because the unnatural link warnings were often the result of tens or hundreds of thousands of bad links to a single site. Google eventually back-tracked and said that these unnatural link warnings may not result in a penalty after all. The word on the street was that Google would be releasing a tool to help webmasters clean up their link profiles.

When you think about it, Google's flip-flopping on this policy was understandable and just. After all, if websites were going to get penalized for having too many spammy links pointing to their pages, then that would open the doors of opportunity to criminal types. Dishonest webmasters looking to take down their competition would simply need to point thousands of low-quality links to their pages using automated link-building software.

In July, Google announced a further 86 changes to its algorithm.

In August, the search engine giant started to penalize sites that had repeatedly violated copyright, possibly via The Digital Millennium Copyright Act (DMCA) takedown requests.

For those who might not be familiar with this, the DMCA is a controversial United States digital rights management (DRM) law. It was first enacted on October 28, 1998, by the then-President Bill Clinton. The intent behind DMCA was to create an updated version of copyright laws. The aim was to deal with the special challenges of regulating digital material.

Ok, moving on to September 2012, another major update occurred, this time called the EMD update. You'll remember that EMD stands for Exact Match Domain and refers to a domain that exactly matches a keyword phrase the site owner wants to rank for. EMDs had a massive ranking advantage simply because they used the keyword phrase in the domain name. This update removed that advantage overnight.

In October of that year, Google announced that there were 65 algorithm changes in the previous two months.

On October 5, there was a major update to Penguin, probably expanding its influence to non-English content.

Also, in October, Google announced the Disavow tool. This was Google's answer to the "unnatural links" problem. It completely shifted the responsibility of unnatural links onto the webmaster by giving them a tool to disavow or deny any responsibility or support for those links. If there were any external links from bad neighborhoods pointing to your site, and you could not get them removed, you could now disavow those links, effectively rendering them harmless.

Finally, in October 2012, Google released an update to its "Page Layout" update. In December, it updated the Knowledge Graph to include non-English queries for the more common languages. This drew an end to the Google updates for that year.

Changes in 2013

In 2013, Google updated both Panda and Penguin several times. These updates refined the two different technologies to try to increase the quality of pages ranking in the SERPs. On July 18, a Panda update was thought to have been released to "soften" the effects of a previously released Panda, so Google obviously watched the effects of its updates, and modified them accordingly.

In June, Google released the "Payday Loan" update. This targeted niches with notoriously spammy SERPs. These niches were often highly commercial, which offered great rewards for any page that could rank highly. Needless to say, spammers loved sites like these. Google gave the example of "payday loans" as a demonstration when announcing this update, hence its name.

August 2013 - Hummingbird - Fast & Accurate?

Hummingbird was the name given to Google's new search algorithm. It was not part of an existing algorithm or a minor algorithm update, but an entirely new algorithm that was unboxed and moved into place on August 20, 2013 (though it was not announced to the SEO community until September 26).

This was a major change to the way Google sorted through the information in its index. In fact, a change on this scale had probably not occurred for over a decade. Think of it this way. Panda and Penguin were changes to parts of the old algorithm, whereas

Hummingbird was a completely new algorithm, although it still used components of the old one.

Google algorithms are the mathematical equations used to determine the most relevant pages to return in the search results. The equation uses over 200 components, including things like PageRank and incoming links, to name just two.

Apparently, the name Hummingbird was chosen because of how fast and accurate these birds were. Although many webmasters disagreed, Google obviously thought at the time that this reflected its search results - fast and accurate.

Google wanted to introduce a major update to the algorithm because of the evolution in the way people used Google to search for stuff. An example Google gave was in "conversation search", whereby people could now speak into their mobile phone, tablet or even desktop browser to find information. To illustrate, let's say that you were interested in buying a Nexus 7 tablet. The old way of finding it online was to type something like this into the Google search box:

"Buy Nexus 7"

However, with the introduction of speech recognition, people have become a lot more descriptive in what they are searching for. Nowadays, it's just as easy to dictate into your search browser something like:

"Where can I buy a Nexus 7 near here?"

The old Google could not cope too well with this search phrase, but the new Hummingbird was designed to do just that. The old Google would look for pages in the index that included some or all the words in the search phrase. A page that included the exact phrase would have the best chance of appearing at the top of Google. If no pages were found with the exact phrase, then Google would look for pages that included the important words from it, e.g. "where" "buy" and "Nexus 7".

The idea behind Hummingbird was that it should be able to interpret what the searcher was *really* looking for. In the example above, they are clearly looking for somewhere near their current location to purchase a Nexus 7.

In other words, Hummingbird was supposed to determine searcher "intent" and return pages that best matched that intent, as opposed to best matching keywords in the search phrase. Hummingbird is still around today and tries to understand *exactly* what the searcher wants, rather than just considering the words used in the search term.

On December 2013, there was a drop in the authorship and rich snippets displayed in the SERPs. This was a feature where Google displayed a photo of the author and/or other information next to the listing. However, Google tightened up its search criteria and removed these features from listings.

Changes in 2014

In February 2014, Google updated its page layout update.

In May the same year, Payday Loan 2.0 was released. This was an update to the original Payday Loan algorithm and was thought to have extended the reach of this algorithm to international queries.

Also in May, Panda was updated. It was called Panda 4.0.

Changes in 2015

The Mobile-friendly Update

On April 21, Google began rolling out an update that was designed to boost mobile-friendly web pages in the mobile search results.

To help webmasters prepare for the update, Google provided a web page where webmasters could test their site to see if it was mobile-friendly or not. You can find the mobile-friendly testing tool here:

https://www.google.com/webmasters/tools/mobile-friendly/

To use this tool, you simply enter your web page URL and wait for the results. Hopefully, you will see something like this:

Tested on: Feb 3, 2020 at 9:56 AM

Page is mobile friendly

This page is easy to use on a mobile device

The mobile-friendly update:

1. Only affects searches carried out on mobile devices.
2. Applies to individual pages, not entire websites.
3. Affects ALL languages globally.

This update makes a lot of sense. If someone is searching on a small screen, Google only wants to show web pages that will display properly on such devices.

Changes in 2016

On the 23rd of February, Google made some big changes to the SERPs, removing the right-hand column of adverts and placing a block of 4 adverts at the top of the SERPs. For any given search term, organic results were now pushed down the page. Above the fold, most searchers only saw the paid advertising links.

On May 12th, Google rolled out a second mobile-friendly update that essentially reinforced the first and made mobile sites perform better on mobile search platforms.

On the 1st of September, another animal joined Google's ranks. The "Possum" update was thought to target local search rankings, increasing the diversity of the local results, but also preventing spam from ranking. Local businesses that had previously found it difficult to rank for a city's results, simply because they were just outside the limits of the city, now found it easier.

On 23rd September, Google announced Penguin 4.0. This was a long-awaited (and anticipated) update by the SEO community. Penguin 4.0 is real-time and a core part of the algorithm. That means that any pages caught by Penguin, can be fixed, and those penalties reversed as soon as the page is re-indexed and reassessed by Penguin. With previous iterations of Penguin, webmasters had to wait months (or even years) to see if their SEO fixes reversed the Penguin penalty.

Changes in 2017

In January, Google started to roll out an update that would impact pages that had intrusive popups or other "interstitials" ruining the mobile experience. Essentially, anything that covered the main content on mobile devices and required attention (e.g. a click) to dismiss it, was targeted.

In April, it appeared that HTTPS websites were favored over the insecure HTTP sites.

In October, Google introduced Google Chrome warnings for insecure websites. That wasn't an algorithm update but I felt it was important bearing in mind what I wrote in the previous paragraph.

We also saw a reduction in the number of featured snippets in the search results, with an increase in knowledge panels.

Changes in 2018

In March 2018, Google rolled out the Mobile-First index. This change meant that instead of indexing desktop versions of pages for the search results, Google started using the mobile versions of the web pages. Why? Because of problems searchers had on mobile devices when the desktop and mobile versions of a page were vastly different.

In July 2018 Google started showing all non-HTTPS sites as "not secure" in the Chrome browser.

In August, Google rolled out a big core update that has been nicknamed the "Medic" update. This update affected a lot of health-related sites (hence the name), especially alternative medicine. There have been suggestions that this update targeted sites that made money by recommending products that could be "dangerous" to health or livelihood.

If you are building affiliate style websites, the Medic update is the single most important reason to stay away from niches related to health & finance. In fact, anything that could be perceived as "risky" to a visitor.

If you have a website in one of these niches and you have been hit by the Medic update, then I am sorry, but I have no simple solution for you. If you search Google, you will find sites that claim to have recovered and those sites would be the best place to start.

Changes in 2019

In 2019, Google released a number of "core" updates. These updates affect a number of ranking factors in one go, so no information was provided on specific targets of the updates.

Just to show that everyone can make mistakes, Google did report a few bugs in April and May. The first was a bug that caused unintentional deindexing of pages. The second stopped new pages from being indexed properly.

Perhaps the biggest news of 2019 was the BERT update. BERT stands for Bidirectional Encoder Representations from Transformers and is a natural language processing (NLP) model. This update aimed to better understand the natural language used by searchers to decide intent and understand the context.

That brings us up to the current time, as I am writing this book. As you can see, Google has been very active in trying to combat the spam thrown at it. The two major updates that changed everything were Panda and Penguin. Together, these two technologies weed out low-quality pages, and pages that have been engineered to rank highly in the search engines.

Anyone who builds a website will want it to rank well in Google. Without having a high-profile presence in the SERPs, a site won't get much traffic, if any at all. If that happens, webmasters WILL try to boost their rankings, and the traditional way is by working on the "on-page SEO" and inbound links. This is where webmasters and Google collide.

Google wants the best pages to rank at the top of the SERPs for obvious reasons. So, Google rewards the pages that deserve to be at the top, rather than pages that webmasters force to the top using SEO (much of which Google collectively calls "Webspam").

What this means to you is that you must deliver the absolute best quality content you can. You need to create content that deserves to be at the top of the SERPs and is likely to attract links from high-quality sites in your niche. Content is not only King now, but it has always been King. The difference now is that Google algorithms are so much better at identifying great content. It's no longer easy to take shortcuts and use underhanded tactics to trick the algorithms as it once was.

That brings us up to date as I write this book. As you can see, Google has been very active in trying to combat the spam thrown at it. Google wants to weed out low-quality pages and undeserving pages that have been engineered to rank highly in the search engines.

Where Does This Leave You?

Anyone that builds a website will want it to rank well in Google because, without that, the site won't get much traffic. Therefore, webmasters WILL try to boost their rankings, and the traditional way is by working on the "on-page SEO" and inbound links. However, over the last couple of years, in particular, Google has introduced measures that try to penalize any webmaster that is actively trying to boost rankings via traditional SEO.

Google wants the best pages to rank at the top of the SERPs. Google wants to reward the pages that deserve to be at the top, rather than the pages that are forced to the top by SEO (much of which Google collectively calls "Webspam").

What this means to you, is that you have to deliver the absolute best quality content you can. You need to create content that deserves to be at the top of Google.

Fortunately, Google does offer us a lot of advice on how to create the type of content it wants in its SERPs. In fact, it has set up a web page called "Webmaster Guidelines" to tell us exactly what it wants, and what it doesn't want. We'll look at this shortly, but first, let's see how we used to create content.

How We Used to Write Content

Let's have a look at how content used to be written. Armed with the knowledge of the previous section, you should be able to easily spot why those techniques no longer work.

I'll show you an example article in a minute – one that used to rank well in Google and was quite profitable through Adsense advertising. First, let me walk you through the process that was used to write the article (the same process millions of webmasters used, and some still do, to create webspam).

Step 1 – Identify profitable keyword phrases.

This was (and still is) fairly easy. Using Google's own keyword tool, webmasters would find as many relevant keywords as they could. Keywords would then be sorted and filtered to find profitable ones. These would have:

- High demand (searched for a lot).
- Low competition (not many competing pages in Google for that term).
- High CPC in Google AdWords.

Step 2 – Write an article focused on a profitable keyword in the hope that it would rank well for that, and usually only that, keyword phrase. The keyword phrase was typically placed in the title, the body of the article a few times (let's say a density of 4%), etc., and a couple of synonyms were added, if possible.

A page created this way had the potential to rank high, and get traffic.

A lot of "Internet Marketers" used this as their business model, creating dozens, even hundreds or thousands of websites (using tools in many cases to automate the site building) with lots of pages targeting individual, high demand phrases. By slapping up several Adsense adverts on their pages, they could monetize that traffic and make money from their websites.

It was not unusual to see a single website, with individual pages built around each of the following keywords:

- Colored contact lenses
- Coloured contact lenses
- Colored contact lens
- Coloured contact lens
- Colored contact lenses online
- Coloured contact lenses online

- Coloured contact lens online
- Colored contact lens online
- Buy colored contact lens
- Buy coloured contact lens
- Buy colored contact lenses
- Buy coloured contact lenses
- Buy colored contact lens online
- Buy coloured contact lens online
- Buy colored contact lenses online
- Buy coloured contact lenses online

All of these articles were essentially about the same thing, just targeting a different keyword phrase. And they all appeared on the same website.

I remember one software tool that made a lot of people very rich. You simply pasted your keyword list (often hundreds of thousands of keywords) into the software, and the software would spit out a website with one page per keyword. Each page would include Adsense ads to make money from visitors. The web page content was actually just Google results for that keyword phrase. Quite clever really, since all pages built by the software were obviously highly relevant to the phrase that was targeted.

As you can imagine, the level of spam in the Google index skyrocketed. It really did seem like the wild west.

Here is a real piece of content that was written well before Panda and Penguin, ranked well, and made a fair bit of money through Google Adsense.

Special Effects Contact Lenses

Have you seen star of the movie Riddick Chronicles? Bet you've wondered for the longest time where to get his obviously special contact lenses. Films and the costume industry need to employ a lot of special effects to make the character more convincing, and special effects contact lenses, help to achieve this look. But special effects contact lenses are medical devices too and that means great care must be used in buying and wearing them.

Since special effects contacts are medical devices, under FDA law, any purchaser must be fitted for them before he or she can use these. Even if you have 20/20, vision or possess a mild case of astigmatism.

23

Examples of special effects lenses are: Wild Eyes Zebra, Pool Shark 8 Ball, Starry eyes (have the stars and moon in your pupils), The Stars & Stripes: an American flag, Red Spiral: red with a white spiral, Fire: yellow flames circle your pupil on a red background or Bloodshot: white with red "blood vessels".

Special effects contacts are made out of soft lenses and worn according to different replacement schedules, such as:

Daily wear lenses - These lenses must be removed at the end of each day, cleaned and then stored.

Extended wear soft lenses - designed to be worn for periods up to a month and can be worn even when sleeping.

Disposable contact lenses – worn for a specified time and then thrown away.

So, whether you just like to show your patriotism during the celebration of Independence Day, or change a mood, special effects contacts can do that for you with punctuation.

However, you must never share or swap your costume contacts with anybody. An eye infection caused by improper use can lead to blindness.

Get fitted for your prescription, for it the contact lenses don't fit your eyes properly, it could lead to serious eye problems, scarring, abrasions and infections.

As long as you follow the rules in buying special effect lenses and take care of the ones you have, you won't have to worry a thing about wearing them. So, make sure you go to a trained eye professional for your contacts.

That is 363 words.

Read it and see what you think.

Is this a good article?

Does it read naturally?

Can you imagine finding an article like that in Google today?

Can you see what phrase the author was trying to rank for?

The webmaster was clearly trying to target the phrase "special effects contact lenses". The article included:

- **Special effects contact lenses** in the title and twice in the opening paragraph.
- **Special effects contacts** THREE times.
- **Special effects** SEVEN times in the article and once more in the title.

Overall:

- **Special** appeared NINE times on the page.
- **Effect(s)** appeared NINE times on the page.
- **Contact(s)** appeared ELEVEN times on the page.
- **Lenses** appeared TWELVE times on the page.

And this was actually one of the better pieces of keyword-focused content that I saw ranking in Google!

This article is clearly very poor. It's not just that it is obviously focused on a specific keyword phrase, the article also suffers from poor grammar throughout. To me, it reads as if someone was given a keyword phrase, and asked to fill in a bunch of words around that phrase ;)

Though badly written, the article isn't all bad. It does actually include some useful information. Overall, though, I am sure you agree that you would not expect to read that article in a newspaper or magazine discussing special effects contact lenses, would you?

Google has actually stated in its guidelines that one of the tests you can apply to your content is whether or not it would be out of place in a quality magazine.

I have a different test for my own content. I ask myself, *would visitors want to share this content?*

In other words, is the content "Share Bait". We'll come back to this term later in the book. For now, I want us to turn our attention to what we know Google wants and does not want.

The Webmaster Guidelines

If you want your pages to rank well in Google, **follow Google's Rules...**

You can find them by searching for **Google Webmaster Guidelines** in Google:

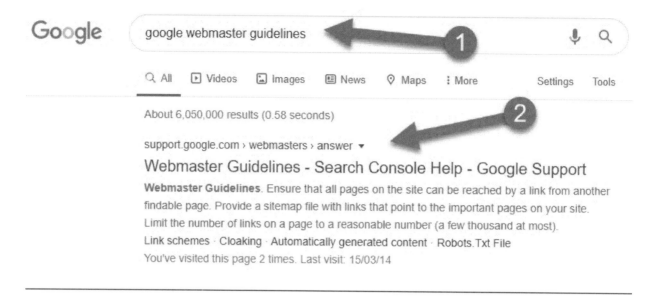

If you don't want to read through all of the guidelines, or this chapter, I can summarize what Google wants in terms of content in just one sentence.

Create the quality content your visitors want to read and don't try to cheat the system.

Google can gauge how successful you are in that goal because it monitors a number of factors including:

- How long a visitor stays on your page/site
- The bounce rate of your pages (the percentage of people that bounce straight back to Google after visiting your page).
- How many citations/shares your page(s) gets from social networks like Twitter, Facebook, and especially Google Plus.

Obviously, content is only one part of the jigsaw puzzle. You can have great content but break some of the other rules in the Webmaster Guidelines. Do that and you are just as likely to lose rankings and disappear from the SERPs. For that reason alone, I recommend you read this chapter in full, and refer back to the Google guidelines regularly, as they are updated occasionally.

A Breakdown of the Google Webmaster Guidelines

The guidelines cover more than just creating good content. They are there to tell you the best ways to help Google "find, crawl and index your site" as well as the "quality" aspects. The guidelines also give specific examples of what Google considers "illicit" practices that could lead to a site being penalized or even removed (de-indexed) from Google.

Let's go through some of the more important points.

Design and Content Guidelines

- **Include a sitemap.** A sitemap should link to the most important pages on your site, in fact, every page that you want Google to know about.
- **Every page on your site should be reachable via at least one link on another findable page.** I'd actually go one step further and suggest that you make sure every page on your site is only two clicks away from the homepage.
- **Create a useful, information-rich site.**
- **Think about words users would type to find your pages, and make sure that your site actually includes those words within it.** This is one instruction that I think is left over from the pre-Panda and pre-Penguin Google. As we saw earlier in the book, a lot of top pages that rank for a phrase do not include that phrase on the page. I think it is important to include all of the words that make up a phrase, but having the exact phrase is unnecessary.
- **Ensure that your alt attributes are descriptive, specific, and accurate.** A lot of webmasters use the ALT tags as a way of inserting more keyword phrases into a page. Don't do it. Not only does Google see this "keyword stuffing" as "Webspam", but it also deprives your blind and visually impaired visitors from accurately "reading" your web page.
- **Design your site to have a clear conceptual page hierarchy.**
- **Use the nofollow tag on advertisement links.**

Quality Guidelines

The quality guidelines cover the more common forms of "deceptive and manipulative behavior" to avoid. However, as Google points out, just because something is not listed in this section, does not mean it is safe. This section is well summarized by this sentence from the quality guidelines.

"Webmasters who spend their energies upholding the spirit of the basic principles will provide a much better user experience and subsequently enjoy better ranking than those who spend their time looking for loopholes they can exploit."

By looking at what not to do, we can get a good idea of what Google actually wants. Many of these things will come as no surprise after we saw the long list of Google algorithm changes earlier.

Before we look at the list of what not to do, Google does offer a few points on what it DOES want us to do. They are:

1. **Make pages primarily for users, not for search engines.** Remember that special effects contact lenses article? Was that written for the user or the search engine? That article is exactly what Google does not want, and writing content by focusing on a specific keyword phrase is only going to cause you problems.
2. **Don't deceive your users.** This is a wide-ranging statement that covers a whole host of sins. We will see examples of this in a moment.
3. **Avoid tricks intended to improve search engine rankings.** Google suggests you ask yourself "Does this help my users? Would I do this if search engines didn't exist?" If the answer is no, don't do it. I certainly would not feel happy showing the special effects contact lens article to a Google employee as an example of my site content, would you?
4. **Think about what makes your website unique, valuable, or engaging. Make your website stand out from others in your field.** This is probably one of the more important things to remember. If you want your page to rank number one in Google, does it deserve to? How is your page better than the pages already ranked in the top 10? What does your page add? What makes it unique and valuable enough that Google has to include it in the top 10?

OK, so those are the guidelines on what Google actually wants. Now let's look at a few examples of things to avoid.

Things Not to Do

1. **Automatically generate content.** This is content that has been created by some form of computer program or script. An example that may seem less obvious is to take your English article and use a software program to convert that in Spanish, German and French, and then post that content on your site to offer your visitors different languages. There is nothing to stop you using a translator tool to create an initial draft in another language, but you must get someone proficient in that language to go through and make changes so that it is actually grammatically correct. Another technology that became popular a few years ago (and is still done by many today), is spinning articles. This is a process whereby one article is spun into different versions using a tool that swaps out synonyms, sentences, and even whole paragraphs.

2. **Link Schemes**. The term "link scheme" covers a multitude of sins, but basically, includes "any links intended to manipulate PageRank or a site's ranking in Google search results". We all know that links help a page to rank in the SERPs. Therefore, webmasters have come up with all manner of "link schemes" to build backlinks, increase their rankings and increase profits. Link schemes include buying/bribing and selling links, link exchanges, large-scale article marketing or guest posting with keyword rich anchor text links, and using automated software to build links. In fact, any link that was not "editorially placed or vouched for by the site's owner" is considered an unnatural link. Remember those?

3. **Cloaking (and sneaky redirects)**. This is a way of deceiving both the visitor and the search engines. One version of a page is shown to the search engines (which is highly optimized to rank well), but when the link in the SERPs is clicked, the user is redirected to a completely different page (which isn't so highly optimized and therefore would not have ranked so well in the search engine).

4. **Hidden text or links**. Using CSS (a technology that helps us control how our web pages look in a browser), it is quite easy to make the text the same color as the background (for example white text on a white background), effectively making it invisible. This was a technique that some people used to stuff keyword phrases into their pages in the hope that their page would rank for those phrases. The search engine spiders would see the keywords since they are viewing a text-based version of the page, but human visitors would not see the keywords. Hidden links were often used to manipulate Page Rank and ultimately rankings.

5. **Doorway pages**. This is still used a lot today. The webmaster sets up a large number of pages, each trying to rank for a specific term. The special effects contact lenses article we saw earlier is a good example of a doorway page. That page was designed to rank for that one keyword, but the site it was found on targeted hundreds of keyword phrases, each one on a separate web page. A twist on the doorway page idea is where all of the doorway pages are on separate websites, and they all link to a single web page or sales letter on a different website. The idea here was to funnel the doorway traffic to a single sales page. This system helped spread the risk, because if one doorway page (and the domain it was on) got penalized, the others were still safely working away, funneling that traffic (and Page Rank) to the main sales page.

6. **Scraped Content**. This is where a webmaster took content from one site and posted it on their own site. Software tools were often employed to do this job. The idea was to increase the amount of content on a website in the hope that this increased the number of terms the site ranked for, therefore bringing in more traffic and increasing profits. While some content scrapers stole complete articles, even entire websites, and therefore infringed copyright, others stayed

within the law and were a little less aggressive. For example, a webmaster might grab videos from YouTube and embed them into pages on his own site. That is within the terms of YouTube, so isn't stealing content. However, just embedding the video in a new web page is not enough to satisfy Google, because the video is already available on YouTube. Why do we need a second copy on the web? The webmaster MUST add significant value to any content "scraped" from another site. In the YouTube video example, this would mean adding original thought, opinion, and commentary on the web page.

7. **Thin affiliate site**s. Affiliate sites can be a great way to make a second (or even primary) income. You place adverts on your site and if someone buys something through your link, you make a commission. However, if you run an affiliate site, you MUST add significant value for your visitor. You cannot just throw up pages and pages of affiliate product "reviews" containing nothing but copied product descriptions, copied reviews, an image or two and an affiliate link. Google wants you to add your own unique and original content to the pages. Google states in its guidelines that "Affiliate program content should form only a small part of the content of your site". Does your site offer anything that the original merchant site does not?

8. **Keyword Stuffing**. This is where a page has words, phrases or numbers added, purely in an attempt to manipulate web page ranking. For example, if you had a website on teeth whitening, and included a list of the US states in the hope of ranking for "teeth whitening California", "teeth whitening Utah", "teeth whitening Kansas", etc., then that is keyword stuffing. Google will penalize you for this.

9. **Preventing and removing user-generated spam**. If you run a Wordpress site, then chances are you'll be accepting comments from visitors. A lot of comments will only be written by people looking for a link back to their own website, and many people use software tools to create hundreds or thousands of comments on any blog that accepts them. Never EVER approve a comment that does not add value to the page on your site. Don't approve comments that attempt to flatter you with "Great site", or "Wow, I learned a lot". They are clearly spam comments that are trying to appeal to your ego to get them approved. If you run any type of site that offers visitors a profile page, or a forum, you need to keep those clean as well. Low-quality profile pages (as generated by spammers and their software tools), as well as spammy forum posts, are YOUR responsibility if they are on your site, and Google will hold you accountable.

10. **Abusing rich snippet markup**. This is the code you can add to your pages to enhance your search results with star ratings or other rich snippets. If Google finds you abusing this, you will get penalized.

That covers the webmaster guidelines. Hopefully, you aren't feeling daunted by that long list of don'ts. As you can see, Google is serious about making its search engine results the best they can be. If you want to see your pages ranking in the SERPs, you need to take these guidelines seriously. It actually isn't that difficult. Just remember a couple of simple rules.

1. Create content for your visitor, not for the search engines.
2. Don't do something you wouldn't otherwise do if search engines didn't exist.

OK, let's look at how we can create content that the search engines will love. To do that, we need to create content that our visitors love, and that means we need content ideas.

What sort of content do your visitors want to see?

Finding Content Ideas

The secret to keeping Google happy is to provide your visitors with the type of content that keeps them engaged, makes them want to come back, and excites them enough that they want to tell their friends, family and social (Twitter, Facebook, etc.) followers about it.

Your first job is to come up with content ideas that can satisfy these rigorous demands.

There are a number of ways to come up with this type of content, and in this chapter, I am going to go through some of the better ones.

1. Check Out Competitor Sites

This is usually my first stop. Do a search on Google for a generic term related to your niche and then visit the top 10 sites to see what they are talking about.

If these sites have social sharing buttons, see which pieces of content have the most shares, as those are the ones that have the potential to excite your audience as well.

2. Use "footprints" to Find Popular Content

This is one of my favorite ways of finding popular topics to write about.

A lot of websites are built using a Content Management System (CMS). A good example of a popular CMS is Wordpress. In fact, I use Wordpress exclusively on all of the websites I run.

One thing you may notice as you look at a lot of Wordpress sites is that certain phrases appear on most or all of the pages of the site. This is because those phrases are hard-coded into Wordpress itself.

A good example can be seen below:

Leave a Reply

Your email address will not be published. Required fields are marked *

See that phrase "Leave a Reply"? That phrase appears on hundreds of thousands of websites built with Wordpress, just above the comments box. If I do a search on Google for "Leave a Reply" in quotes, this is what I get:

Google tells me that there are "about 566 million" pages that have that exact phrase on the page.

Now, in terms of finding content ideas, this footprint is not very useful. However, there is a related footprint that is pure gold.

Check out this screenshot:

A lot of websites allow visitors to comment. The page above has 1,395 comments!

So how can we use this as a "footprint" to find popular content? We can't search for "1,395 comments"!

Using a little trick of the trade, we can modify the number component of a search term, to include a number range like this:

"50..500 comments"

If you search for this in Google, the search engine returns pages that have anywhere from 50 to 500 comments. Cool eh?

I've used 50..500 as my number range, but you could change this to 100..1000 or whatever you want. It will all depend on your niche and how many results Google is finding for your footprints. In less popular niches, you may need to reduce your lower limit to something like 20 or 25.

Now, the footprint we've just talked about isn't much use on its own. We need to tell Google that we are only interested in pages related to our niche. Let's look at a specific example.

Let's say I have a website on weight loss.

I would select a few generic keyword phrases for my niche like "weight loss", "lose weight", "lose fat" and maybe even "diet", and then build footprints, like this:

"50..500 comments" "weight loss"

"50..500 comments" "lose weight"

"50..500 comments" "lose fat"

"50..500 comments" "diet"

I would then visit Google and type these into the search box. Let's take one of those strings and run it through Google now.

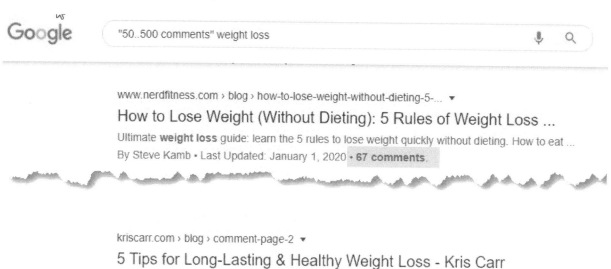

Google uses our search string in the listing description where possible, so we can instantly see that these results have 67, 163, and 65 comments respectively.

Those are the number of comments to the original post, and represent visitor interaction on the site. Not only could you go to these popular posts and leave your own comments, which would raise awareness for your own website, but you could also check out the topic of the post, work out why it is so interesting to those visitors, and write a similar post on your own site.

Here's an idea.

If a post is a little controversial, why not write an opposing view on your own site and then post a comment on this original post mentioning your opposing view with a link. Assuming your comment was approved, that would not only provide a link to your site but also give you potential visitors interested in seeing your opinions on the topic. People who commented on the original post are more likely to comment on your post, whether they agree or disagree with your point of view. Since Google loves to see posts with comments, that will kick-start your own rankings.

You could use this type of footprint technique to build up sections on your website, or even find complete niche website ideas!

3. Forums

Forums are always a great place to find content ideas, after all, people visit forums to discuss ideas and ask for answers to their problems.

You could start off with a simple Google search like:

"weight loss" "forum"

By enclosing both parts of the search string in quotes, Google will only return pages that have both of those strings on the page.

Here is that search in Google:

Over46 million pages contain the phrase "weight loss" and the word "forum". That's quite a good start and will be good enough for most popular niches. However, that search does not guarantee that the results are actual forums, just that the word "forum" appears on the page.

To increase your chances of finding real forums in your niche, you can again use footprints. Forums are created using scripts, and scripts leave footprints that we can target.

Here are some footprints to try in combination with your generic niche term:

"weight loss" "viewtopic"

"weight loss" "Powered by PHPbb"

"weight loss" "Powered by vBulletin"

There are other footprints, but these should be enough to get you started.

When you get to the forums, look to see what questions people are asking. If there is a question with a lot of replies or obvious interest, consider writing an article for your site on that topic, then join the forum and direct people to your post. Normal forum etiquette means you should not be joining a forum just to link to pages on your own site, you'll be seen as a spammer. But if you join relevant forums, post helpful responses to questions, and ask interesting questions to interact with others, you will eventually be able to link to articles on your own site (or any other site) without being seen as a spammer.

Another footprint that can yield good results is the word "community". After all, communities are groups of like-minded people discussing a topic of interest.

This won't always give you real communities, but it usually does turn up some gems that you can mine for content ideas.

4. Q & A Sites

What better place to find ideas for content than websites set up to ask and answer questions? There are several sites like this, including:

- Answer the Public (https://answerthepublic.com/)
- Yahoo Answers (https://answers.yahoo.com/)
- Quora (https://www.quora.com/).

Quora is my personal favorite. You can type in just about anything at Quora, to find real questions & answers.

Sign up for Quora (it's free), and you can start to join the community and offer help to others. It's a great way to drum up some interest in your website.

There is a search box at the top of the screen, where you can type in your topic of interest:

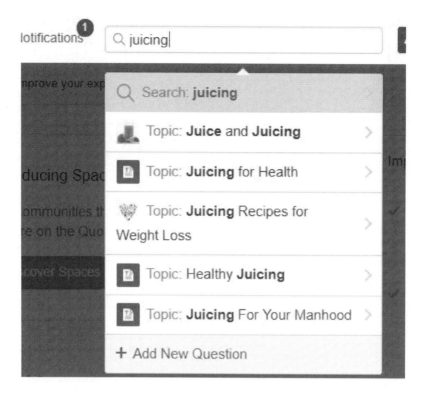

As you start typing, you'll see the auto-complete box drop down so you can select a topic you are interested in.

You'll find a lot of content ideas for your own site just by searching and exploring on Quora.

5. Follow RSS feeds

An RSS feed is essentially a list of pages on a website. RSS feeds can include all pages on a site, or just the last 10 or so pages (the exact number can be controlled by the webmaster).

A lot of websites publish RSS feeds, and in fact, ALL Wordpress sites create RSS feeds automatically. A Wordpress site actually creates a number of different RSS feeds, including feeds for:

- The latest posts
- Each category
- Every tag page
- All posts by each author
- And more...

One of the best ways to find content ideas is to follow competitor websites, and see what content they are publishing. If they publish an RSS feed, it's easy to spy on them.

There are a number of services that can help you monitor the RSS feeds of other websites. My favorite is called Feedly, and you can sign up for a free account at Feedly.com by logging in with your Twitter, Facebook or Google Plus account.

Essentially you tell Feedly the URLs of the RSS feeds that you are interested in, and they'll keep those feeds updated in your account, so you can see the new content as it is published.

Let's do a real example.

Let's suppose I am interested in weight loss.

I can do a search at Google for weight loss RSS feeds as follows:

"weight loss" "rss"

This will find pages that include the phrase "weight loss", but also contain the word "RSS" on the page. This usually returns pages for sites that offer an RSS feed. Here are the results in Google.

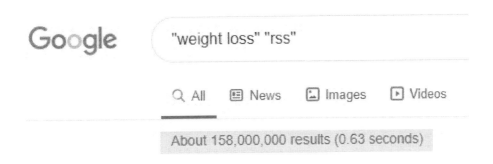

If I click on an item, I can search for an RSS feed which often looks like this:

Rather than click the icon, I typically right click and copy the URL so I can add it to an RSS feed manager.

Log in to Feedly.

To add your copied feed to Feedly, click the **Add Content** button at the bottom of the left sidebar and paste in the RSS feed URL you copied:

.. and click the **Sources** link. You'll see the feed listed:

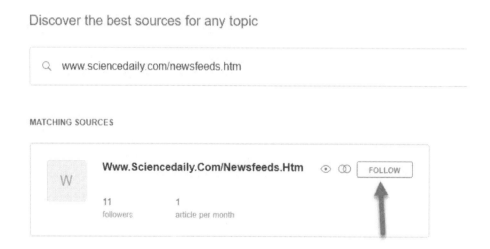

You just need to click on the **Follow** button and you'll now get updates when that site adds new content.

Find a number of RSS feeds and add them all to the same Feedly account.   You can then track new content across a number of sites. You can even let Feedly find feeds for you by entering a keyword and hitting Return.   This will then list a number of relevant feeds that you can easily add to your Feedly account by clicking the follow button.

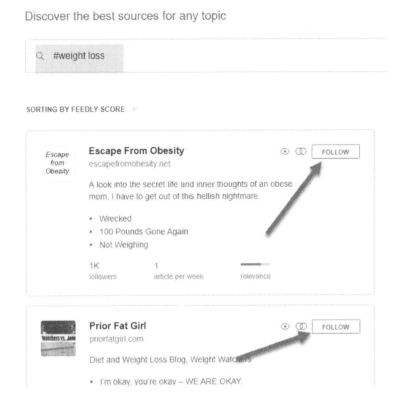

Incidentally, I typed in "weight loss" and Feedly added the hash in front.

Within Feedly you can even create categories to add feeds to, so you could have a category for all "weight loss" feeds, another for "weight loss recipes", another for "diets" and so on. That way you can monitor multiple topics related to your site.

When new content is found in the feeds you are monitoring, you'll see them in your Feedly stream. You can then visit these articles, check out their popularity (social shares, comments, etc), and "borrow" popular topics to write about for your own site.

I'll leave you to explore Feedly yourself, but I'd recommend you certainly add relevant feeds from your competitors, as well as those sites at the top of the search engines for key phrases you want to rank for.

Before we leave the topic of RSS feeds, there is a special case that I wanted to mention – news feeds.

Let's take the weight loss example again.

Over on Google, you need to sign into your Google account (your Gmail account if you have one, if not, create one).

OK, if I search for weight loss, I get this:

Notice that the menu underneath the search box? One of those items is "News", and by clicking it, you can find relevant, up to the minute (usually) news on your chosen search phrase.

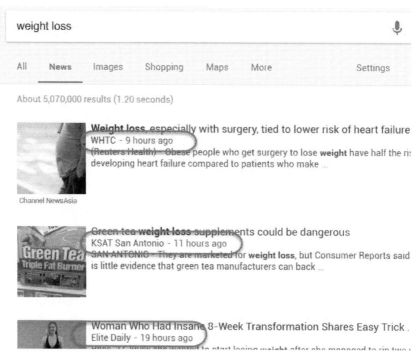

You can see that the first item was posted 9 hours previously, and the next one 11 hours before I searched. That's pretty up-to-date, and if you have a section on your site to show "current news" in your niche, this information can be invaluable.

Google News used to offer an RSS feed for these results pages, but it stopped doing that. However, if you scroll to the bottom of the page, you should see a button to "Create Alert".

Click it.

If you are logged into Google, it will try to create an email alert, like this:

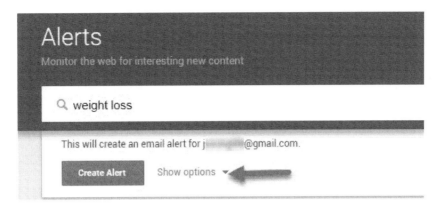

Click the **Show Options** link.

The options panel will open, with an **Alert Preview** screen below.

Check to make sure the preview shows the kind of stories you are interested in.

Make sure you select **RSS feed** in the **Deliver to** box:

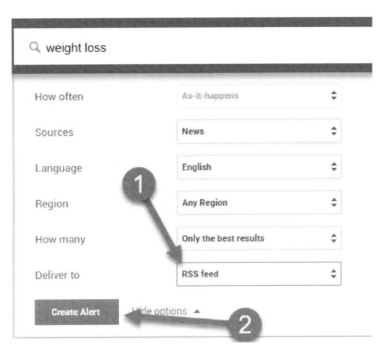

Now click the **Create Alert** button.

Google will now show you a list of all alerts that you have set up.

My alerts (1)

weight loss

Click the feed icon and then copy the URL from your browser address bar.

You can now paste this URL into Feedly to monitor Google news for niche related stories.

Feedly and RSS feeds can keep you up-to-date in your niche, and you'll always hear about the hot topics as they arise. This can be a great way to identify content ideas that are sure to keep your visitors happy.

6. Keyword Research - Using Google Keyword Planner

I was a little reluctant to talk about keyword research tools as a way of finding content ideas, for one simple reason. Armed with the data from a keyword research session, the temptation to create "Webspam" is too hard to resist for many. Keyword research tools are one of the main reasons Google has had to go to extreme measures to clean up its search results of poor, thin content.

For years, the process employed by many internet marketers was the same:

1. Do keyword research.
2. Find keywords that are searched for a lot, have low competition and are commercial terms that are expensive to advertise on Google Ads.
3. Write a page of content around each of these profitable keywords.
4. Slap up Google Adsense on the page.

That was the recipe for many people to make big money online. A single web page ranking high in Google could make 10s or even 100s of dollars a day with Google Adsense clicks. You can see why the temptation was there to get as many pages online as possible, and some webmasters literally put up millions.

With that said, keyword research is still a valuable way to find out what people want. Like so many things, it's how you use the data that will decide whether Google sees you as a great content creator or web spammer.

Google's own keyword research tool is free to use, but it does have the odd annoyance. I'll show you how to overcome those.

Firstly, Google wants users of its keyword tool to use its advertising platform (Google Ads). Therefore, you may find it difficult to sign up without being forced into creating ads or entering a credit card. Don't panic, here are the instructions to sign up without having to create ads or add a credit card.

IMPORTANT: Please note that if you have already gone through the process of setting up a Keyword Planner account using your current email address, you are stuck and will need to create an ad campaign to use the planner. The solution is to create a brand new Gmail address and use that instead.

Set Up a Keyword Planner Account Without an AdWords Campaign

Search Google for Google Keyword Planner and you should find it easily enough:

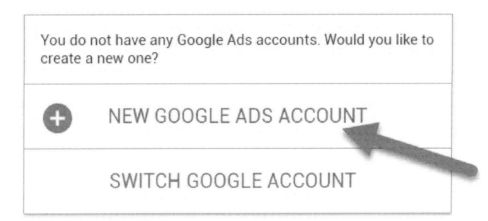

When you land on that page, you will be asked to log in to your Google account. If you are already logged into your account, just click the **Sign In** link top right and you'll be automatically signed in.

On the next screen, click the **New Google Ads Account button:**

Google will then ask you what your main advertising goal is. Under the three main options, look for the link to **Switch to Expert Mode**.

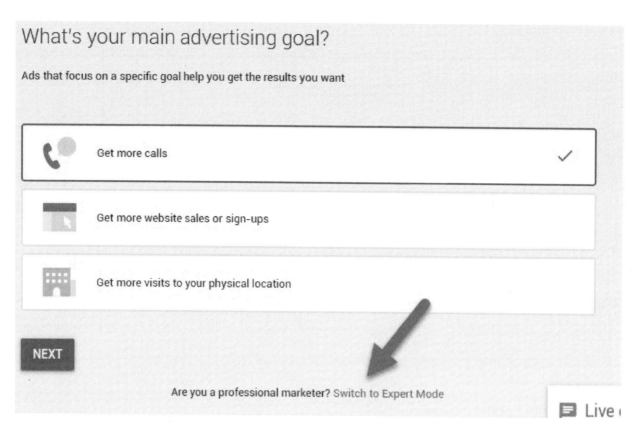

On the next screen, Google will ask you for your goal that would make the campaign successful. Don't click any of those options. Scroll to the bottom and click the link to **Create an account without a campaign:**

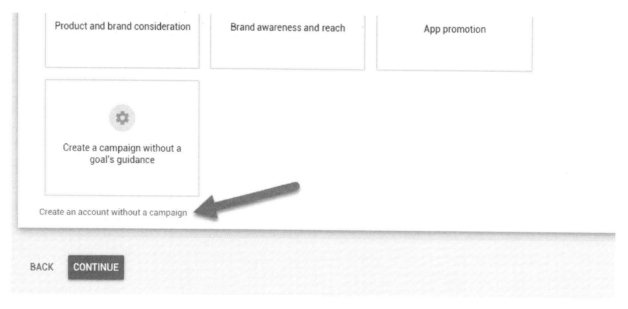

On the next screen, click the **Submit** button:

Confirm your business information

This information will be used to create your account. You can't change these settings later, so choos

📖   Billing country
United Kingdom ▼

🕐   Time zone
(GMT) United Kingdom Time ▼

💳   Currency
British Pound (GBP £) ▼

SUBMIT ⬅

And now click the **Explore Your Account** button.

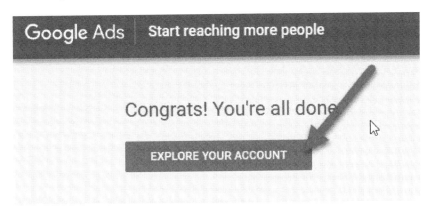

You are taken into your account. To start the Keyword Planner, click on the **Tools & Settings** menu and choose **Keyword Planner** from the **Planning** sub-menu menu.

47

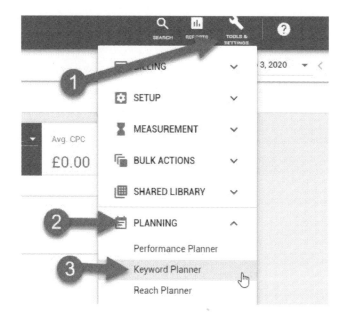

Let's take Keyword Planner for a spin.

Load up the Keyword Planner, and let's see what it can (and cannot) do. On the opening screen, click the **Discover new keywords** button:

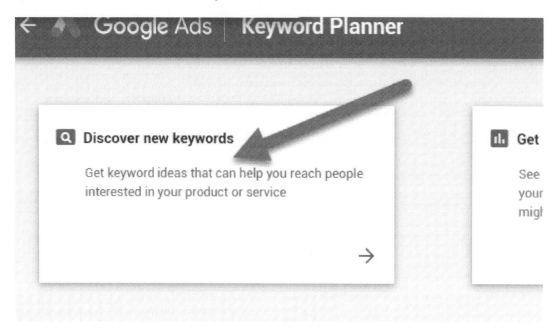

Enter a keyword that you want to explore, and click the button to get started.

Let's assume that I have a technology site and I want to write some articles about the **Samsung Note 9**. That is the term I entered as my search term.

Keyword (by relevance) ↓	Avg. monthly searches	Competition
galaxy note 9	10K – 100K	High
samsung note	1K – 10K	High
samsung galaxy n...	1K – 10K	High
galaxy note	1K – 10K	High
note 9 deals	1K – 10K	High

Google Keyword Planner found 708 keywords related to this term.

You can click any column header to order your results by that column. Since we are looking for high demand keywords, let's order our keywords by average monthly searches (click that column header).

Keyword	↓ Avg. monthly searches	Competition
note 9	10K – 100K	High
note 9 price	1K – 10K	High
samsung s9 note	1K – 10K	High
samsung note 9 pr...	1K – 10K	High
galaxy note	1K – 10K	High

But those demand figures...

This brings us to the second major issue with the Google Keyword Planner. Average monthly searches is a range and a wide range at that.

But I have a fix for that too. It isn't a free fix, but it is a very cheap fix.

Users of Google Chrome and Firefox can install an extension called Keyword Everywhere. Not only does this fix the Keyword Planner range issue, but it gives us some very powerful tools.

Do a Google search for the **Keyword Everywhere** extension and install it for your web browser of choice. You'll need to enter an email address during the install, and Keywords Everywhere will send you an email link to get your API key. You'll need the API key to use their software.

Once installed, you'll have a new button in the toolbar of your browser. That button opens up a menu, and an on/off switch so you can turn the extension off when not being used.

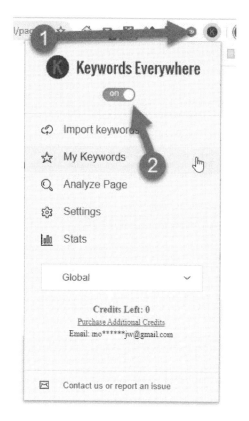

Turn the plugin on, and go into the Settings.

In the API key box, paste in the API key they gave you and click on the **Validate** button. Have a look through the available options and make your selections.

Once done, you can close the Keywords Everywhere settings.

Click on the Keywords Everywhere button in the toolbar again. You'll see that you have 0 credits, so you need to buy some.

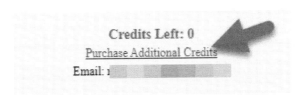

Click the link and you'll be taken to a screen where you can buy credits, where one credit reveals the data on one keyword:

You can get 100,000 credits for just $10.

After buying some credits, head back to the Google Keyword Planner. Log out and then back in again.

Repeat the search you did earlier. Do you notice the difference?

Keyword (by relevance)	Vol	CPC	Comp	Avg. monthly searches
samsung note 9 ⭐	1,900	$1.30	0.93	10K – 100K
note 9 ⭐	3,890	$1.19	0.75	10K – 100K
galaxy note 9 ⭐	200	$1.63	0.99	10K – 100K
samsung galaxy note 9 ⭐	910	$0.88	0.99	10K – 100K
samsung 9 ⭐	3,210	$1.34	0.98	1K – 10K
samsung galaxy note ⭐	201,000	$0.53	0.94	1K – 10K
samsung galaxy 9 ⭐	1,000	$1.30	1	1K – 10K

You've still got the same columns you had before, but you also have three new ones added by Keywords Everywhere.

Vol - The number of monthly searches made for that keyword.

CPC - The cost per click of that keyword.

Comp - A number between 0 (easy) and 1 (hard) for the competition you will face if you want to rank for that keyword.

Keywords Everywhere has added back the detail that Google stripped out in previous updates to the keyword planner.

A great option you have with Keywords Everywhere is to save all of the keyword data to your "favorites". Look at the lower right of the screen:

You'll get this button on all screens that show Keywords Everywhere data (we'll come on to these in a moment). Notice also that you can save the data as a CSV file, meaning easy import into Excel or a similar spreadsheet program.

If you do click **Add All Keywords**, you'll only get those keywords that are currently visible, so scroll to the bottom of the page and select 500 from the **Show Rows** option. You can then scroll through fewer pages of keywords to add them all to your favorites.

To view your keyword data, select **My Keywords** from the menu:

The Keyword table will open, showing you all of the keywords you have added. The columns can be ordered by clicking the column title. So, for example, you can see which keywords cost the most for advertisers:

	Keyword	Volume	CPC	Competition	Volume (US)
☐	upcoming samsung galaxy note	10	$15.12	0.16	10
☐	samsung galaxy release date	1,300	$6.48	0.17	720
☐	samsung note phone release dates	40	$6.23	0.42	30
☐	note 9 release date	49,500	$5.53	1	1,000
☐	galaxy 9 note release date	260	$5.21	1	170
☐	galaxy note release	70	$4.98	0.55	50
☐	the galaxy 9	210	$4.94	0.99	170

The Keyword Planner is Only the Beginning

I can see from the data on Google's Keyword Planner that there is a huge demand for content on the Samsung Note 9. However, I want to get a better idea of what type of content might be in demand. Keywords Everywhere can come to the rescue again. It doesn't just work with Keyword Planner. It also adds keyword data to a lot of other tools, like Google Search:

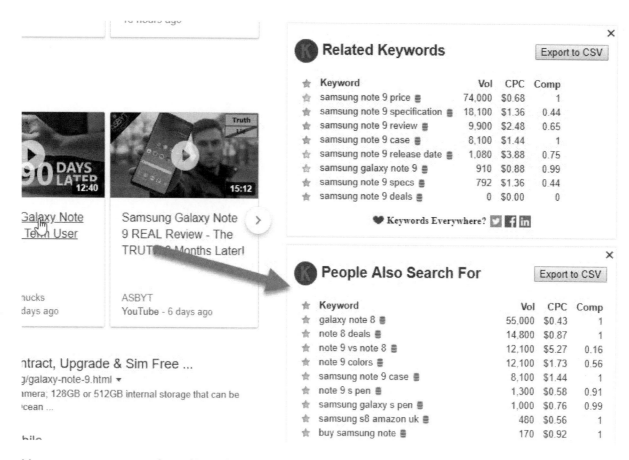

You can see a complete list of sites that get the Keywords Everywhere treatment in the settings screen:

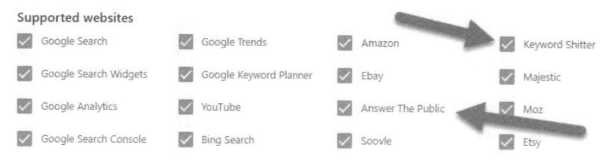

As you can see, this plugin will add keyword data into your Google Analytics and Google Console screens. However, there are two that I really like when doing keyword research. They are called **Keyword Shitter** and Answer the Public. Do a Google search to find them.

Keyword Shitter spits out keywords at a rapid pace, and Keywords Everywhere provides useful data about each phrase. Go and try it.

Here is a snapshot of the phrases returned from that tool:

```
970 - 1544
samsung note 9 flip cover case
samsung note 9 credit card case
samsung note 9 case designer
samsung note 9 case disney
samsung note 9 case drop test
samsung note 9 digital case
samsung note 9 otterbox defender case
samsung galaxy note 9 case otterbox defender
samsung galaxy note 9 heavy duty case
whitestone dome samsung galaxy note 9 case
samsung note 9 case etsy
esr samsung galaxy note 9 case
element case samsung note 9
samsung note 9 case from samsung
samsung note 9 case flip
samsung note 9 case for sale
samsung note 9 folio case
samsung note 9 fabric case
samsung note 9 carbon fiber case
samsung note 9 case jb hi fi
samsung galaxy note 9 folio case
best case for samsung note 9
case for samsung galaxy note 9
otterbox case for samsung note 9
leather case for samsung note 9
lifeproof case for samsung note 9
```

I actually stopped the tool after a minute or so as it keeps on finding new words. I also filtered out only those phrases that contain the word Samsung. So that's 970 keyword phrases that might be useful.

Keywords Everywhere works hard on that page too, finding all the supply and demand data. You can see that as you scroll down the page:

```
samsung note 9 [1,900/mo - $1.30 - 0.93] ☆
samsung note 9 price [33,100/mo - $1.07 - 0.93] ☆
samsung note 9 case [170/mo - $0.68 - 1] ☆
samsung note 9 review [3,600/mo - $2.87 - 0.37] ☆
samsung note 9 deals [0/mo - $0.00 - 0] ☆
samsung note 9 specs [433/mo - $1.71 - 0.31] ☆
samsung note 9 price uk [0/mo - $0.00 - 0] ☆
samsung note 9 ee [0/mo - $0.00 - 0] ☆
samsung note 9 release date uk [0/mo - $0.00 - 0] ☆
samsung note 9 contract [0/mo - $0.00 - 0] ☆
samsung note 9 fortnite [0/mo - $0.00 - 0] ☆
samsung note 9 vodafone [40/mo - $0.83 - 0.78] ☆
```

One thing I like to do with keyword lists like the one from Keyword Shitter is to collect them all in a text file and use Google Keyword Planner to analyze them for CPC, impressions and potential clicks. In other words, get Google to tell me which of the keywords are the most commercial in nature.

Let's see how this works. To demonstrate, I'll grab those 970 keywords from the Keyword Shitter.

On the Keyword Planner site, go up to the Tools menu and select Keyword Planner to start a new session. From the opening screen, select **Get search volume forecasts**:

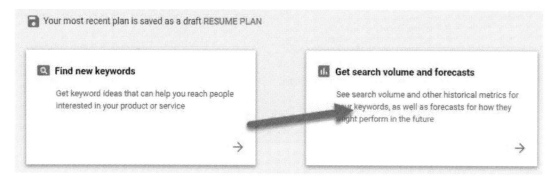

Now paste in the keywords from Keyword Shitter and click **Get Started**:

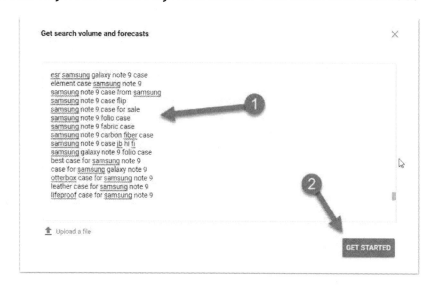

Google Keyword Planner will now go away and find data about your keywords:

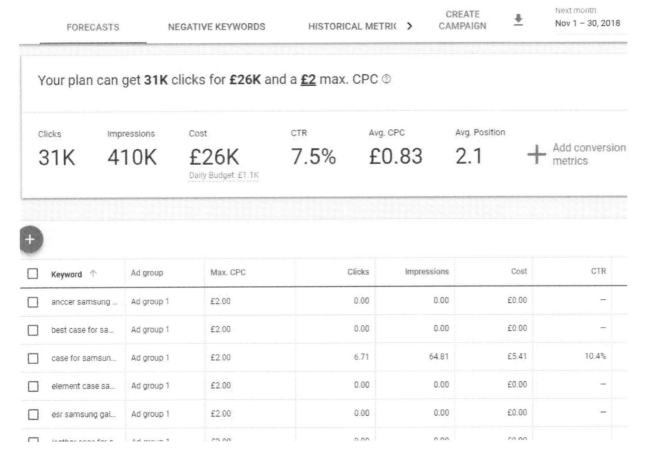

The data in the table is designed for AdWords advertisers, so it provides data about the potential cost per click, CTR, Impressions, etc. of these keywords. This can be very interesting data to look through as it highlights the more commercial keywords (the ones advertisers are already bidding on).

Answerthepublic.com

This is a great tool for finding content ideas and it works with Keywords Everywhere. A quick search for Samsung Note 9 returned keywords in three categories: Questions, Prepositions, and Comparisons.

This tool found 50 questions that people ask about the Samsung Note 9:

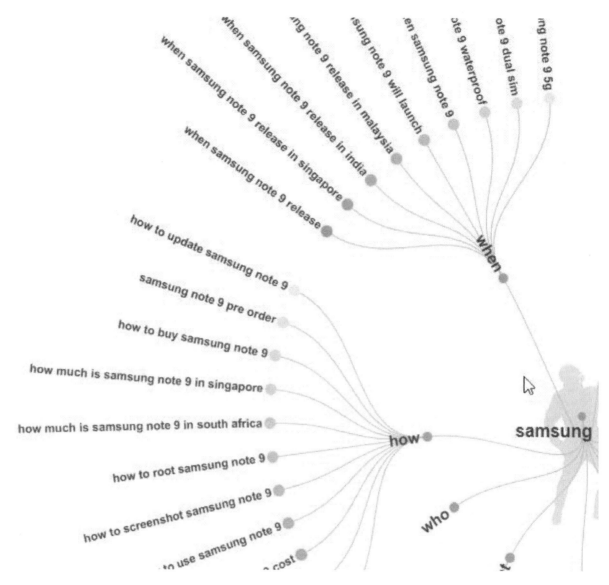

I love these visual diagrams, but you can see the data as plain text if you prefer by switching from **Visualization** to **Data**:

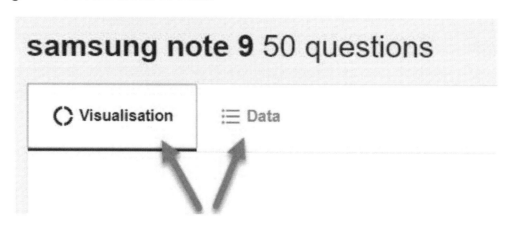

You'll see tables of keywords:

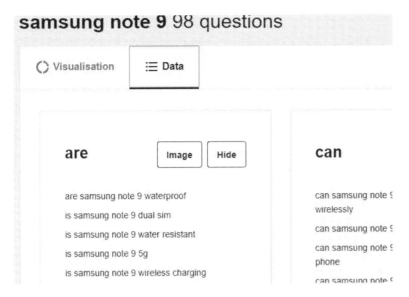

Some of these questions provide excellent ideas for articles on the phone and represent real questions asked by real searchers.

The prepositions section provides further content ideas. These are search phrases about the Samsung Note 9 that include words like can, to, without, near, with, for, and is.

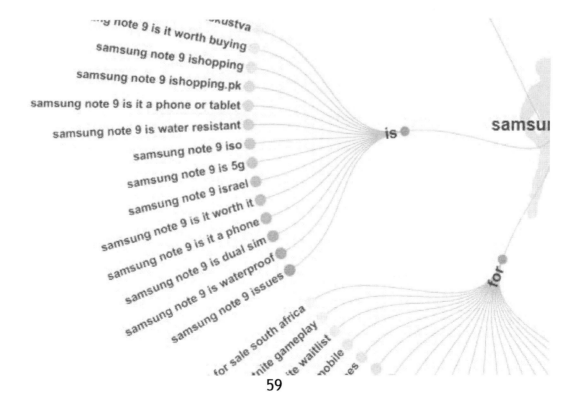

The final section is the comparisons. This again can be pure gold if you are looking for content ideas. These are search phrases that include words like versus, and, like, vs, and or:

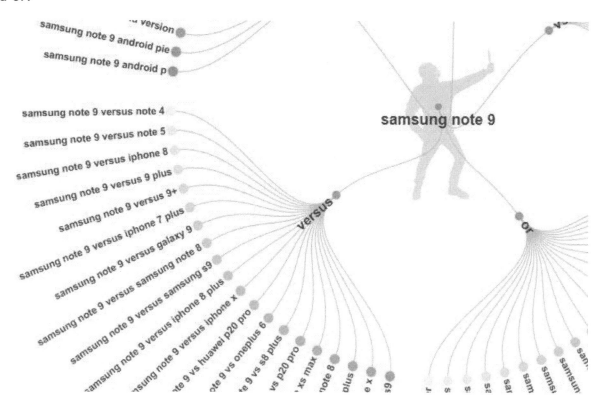

So where does Keywords Everywhere come into all this? Well keep scrolling down and you'll see a list of all keywords at the bottom of the page:

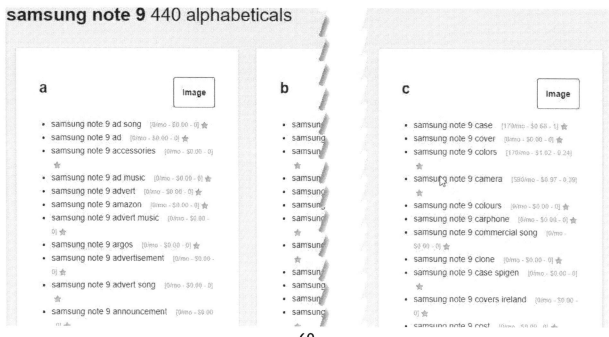

And don't forget that **Add All Keywords** button at the bottom of the page if you want to save all of this data.

Another Keyword Planner Example - Weight Loss

Let's pretend we are in the weight loss niche and looking for content ideas with the Keyword Planner. If necessary, click on the Tools menu and select Keyword Planner to get started. Make sure Keywords Everywhere is running.

Click on the **Find new keywords** button and enter **weight loss** in the search box. Click the **Get Started** button to retrieve keywords.

At the very top of the table, I can see the exact phrase that I typed in:

Keyword (by relevance)	Vol	CPC	Comp
weight loss ☆	368,000	$1.92	0.91
how to lose weight ⁕	450,000	$1.07	0.33
how to lose weight...	450,000	$1.52	0.83
lose weight ☆	246,000	$1.71	0.57

The exact term "weight loss" is searched between 368,000 times per month according to Keywords Everywhere. I can also see that competition is high (lots of advertisers bidding on this phrase) at 0.91 (this is a value between 0 and 1). The average CPC is $1.92.

What does that mean?

If someone searches Google for "weight loss" and Google shows my advert, it wants me to agree to pay up to $1.92 if that person clicks on my ad. That's $1.92 PER CLICK!

Ads can appear in the search results, or on partner sites (and pretty much anyone can be a partner through the AdSense program). Imagine you had a weight loss site and added AdSense to monetize it. If there are advertisers willing to pay $1.92 per click, then every time a visitor to your site clicked this type of advert, you would make a "commission" equal to the lion's share of up to $1.92. Can you see why people started creating pages around specific keyword phrases?

There are a lot of other keywords in this niche that could potentially pay a lot more per click:

Keyword	Volume	CPC	Con
most healthy way to lose weight	30	$11.98	
before after weight loss	5,400	$11.10	
surgical weight loss	720	$10.31	
weight loss surgery	49,500	$9.94	
weight loss camp for adults	1,600	$9.75	
medical weight loss programs	1,300	$9.36	
dotties weight loss	590	$9.10	
healthy ways to lose weight quickly	90	$8.44	
weight loss programs for men	1,900	$8.18	
effective weight loss program	320	$8.06	
weight loss retreat	2,900	$7.27	
dotties weight loss zone	2,400	$6.93	

Can you see why focusing on specific keywords can be so tempting?

You will see a lot of keyword ideas generated by Google. These keywords are taken straight from Google's keyword database, and let's face it, Google knows what people are searching for, so while the data is not 100% accurate (Google would never want to give us all the facts), they are reliable enough to determine in-demand topics.

Looking down the keywords I've generated and filtered for "weight loss", I can see a few good content ideas:

1. Fast weight loss / Rapid weight loss (always popular in the pre-summer months).
2. Weight loss supplements (though this could be a whole category of content on a weight loss site, with different articles exploring different supplements). We also have weight loss pills related to this search.
3. Weight loss surgery.
4. Diet Plans (again this could be a major category on a weight loss site).

5. Diets that work.
6. Medical weight loss gets a lot of searches, though there will be a lot of related search phrases like gastric surgery, gastric bypass, bariatric surgery, etc.

If you find an area that you would like to look into further, just change the search term at the top of the page. You can enter several words if you like:

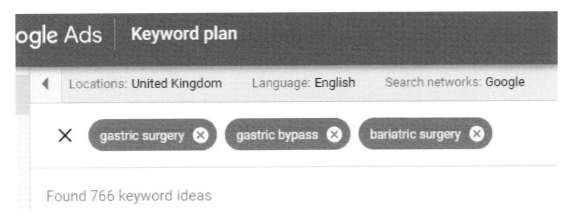

When you click the **Get Results** button, you'll get to see the data for those specific phrases:

	Keyword	Vol	CPC	Comp
☐	obesity surgery centre ☆	40	$2.45	0.54
☐	weight loss surgery houston ☆	480	$37.00	0.85
☐	bypass surgery procedure ☆	720	$0.81	0.09
☐	laparoscopic weight loss surgery ☆	140	$5.07	0.66
☐	laparoscopic gastric bypass ☆	720	$12.80	0.23
☐	gastric bypass and pregnancy ☆	320	$6.96	0.15

.. as well as all of the related terms generated by the Google keyword tool.

This new set gives me more ideas for content, like:

	Keyword	Volume	CPC
☐	gastroplasty	1,900	$16.28
☐	does gastric bypass work	90	$15.52
☐	weight loss surgery before and after	720	$14.01
☐	weight loss surgery financing	260	$12.26
☐	most effective weight loss surgery	140	$11.13
☐	gastric bypass definition	590	$10.15
☐	sleeve surgery	12,100	$9.49
☐	types of gastric bypass surgery	260	$9.00
☐	cheap gastric bypass surgery	90	$8.64

Look at those CPCs!

Each of these phrases on their own could be the inspiration behind an article. It is important to remember, though, that you **WILL NOT** be writing an article targeting the keyword phrase itself. These phrases are just the seeds for content ideas. You need to get inside the head of the person typing these phrases into Google and decide why they are typing the phrase?

For example, looking at all of the keywords that mention "complications" is interesting:

Found 26 keyword ideas

Show broadly related ideas   Exclude adult ideas ✕   Keyword text contains complication ✕   Keyw

Add filter

Keyword	Vol	CPC	Comp
bariatric surgery complications ☆	880	$4.36	0.29
sleeve gastrectomy complications ☆	390	$2.95	0.11
gastric sleeve complications ☆	2,400	$8.19	0.34
gastric bypass surgery complications ☆	390	$8.02	0.35
gastric bypass complications ☆	1,300	$5.99	0.2
gastric band complications ☆	260	$3.29	0.23
complications after gastric bypass surgery ☆	70	$6.95	0.3
roux en y gastric bypass complications ☆	390	$5.72	0.18
lap band complications ☆	590	$3.04	0.24

I'd imagine (though I could be wrong), that the people searching for this phrase are likely to be the potential patients or their families/friends trying to be prepared for all eventualities. In other words, how safe is it? Are complications common?

My initial idea for content might be to find real people who had been through the operation and interview them about the procedure. With the internet, it is relatively easy to find people who are happy to talk and share experiences.

I'd ask them things like:

- How did the operation go?
- How long was the recovery time?
- What, if anything went wrong?
- How have you found eating since the operation?
- Any words of warning to prospective patients?

- If there was one thing you wished you'd known before the operation, what would it be?

I'd be tempted to find some people that were very happy with the operation and the results, and others that had problems. You could put both sides of the story forward, and offer statistics on how likely someone was to face complications.

So, I started with a keyword phrase idea of **gastric bypass complications**.

That is where my approach differs from a lot of old-school SEOs.

Rather than try to rank for that specific phrase as they would, I used the phrase as an idea for a piece of content and wrote about the TOPIC.

My article is likely to rank for that exact phrase (as well as hundreds of other phrases), even if I don't necessarily have the exact phrase on my page. Why? Because the way we theme pages will mean we are including all of the related theme words and phrases that Google expects to see in an authoritative article on that topic. Not only that but with such an interesting and visitor-focused article, it is likely to get a lot of shares and backlinks, which in turn will help it rank.

So, forget the old ways of writing keyword-focused content.

Find phrases that people are looking for, and then try to get into their heads to find out why they are searching for those phrases. Once you can answer that, you can create content that will compete in Google, excite your visitors, attract likes, shares, and most importantly, backlinks!

7. Paid Services

I wanted to briefly touch on a paid service that can help you find in-demand content ideas. It's found at Buzzsumo.com.

Here is a screenshot from that tool showing the results when I searched for cholesterol:

	Facebook Engagement	Twitter Shares	Pinterest Shares	Reddit Engagements	Number of Links	Evergreen Score	Total Engagement				
☐ Select All											
Eggs linked to increased **cholesterol**, risk of heart disease in new study By Alexandria Hein - Mar 15, 2019 foxnews.com	81K	85	4	5	11	5	81K				
Eggs and **cholesterol**: Experts weigh new guidance on eggs, **cholesterol** and heart health By Ashley Welch - Mar 15, 2019 cbsnews.com	76.7K	231	15	11	18	5	77K				
White meat is just as bad for you as red beef when it comes to your **cholesterol** level, study says By Susan Scutti - Jun 4, 2019 cnn.com	72.2K	2.1K	2	34	57	5	74.3K				

This tool will highlight the content that has received the most attention on social media. It's great for finding the next hot topic for your site but you really do need the paid version to get the most out of it. Be warned though, Buzzsumo is quite expensive.

OK, this chapter should have given you lots of ideas on how to find interesting and stimulating content. Remember your main goal. You want to create content that your visitors want to read, and share.

Types of Web Content

Your content should excite, entertain and/or inform your visitors. It should give your visitors what they came for when they started their search at Google.

With any content that you post on your site, it often helps to think whether or not that content would be something your visitors would want to share with their friends or social media followers. This is a good indicator of the type of quality you should be aiming for.

Ultimately the content on your site will determine whether or not your site succeeds in the long term. Do people bookmark your site? Does your content have a lot of social shares? Does your site offer its visitors a unique experience not found on competing websites?

It doesn't matter if your site is a personal project, an eCommerce site, an affiliate site, or a company website. It MUST offer visitors a reason to return and that starts with the content on the site. In this chapter, I hope to give you some ideas to get your creative juices flowing. However, before we look at different types of content, I want to talk briefly about link bait.

Link Bait?

Link bait is a term that you may already know. Essentially, link bait is any type of content that was created to attract links back to the page. Link bait can be something topical, funny or controversial.

To explode your traffic, you need high quality, natural backlinks. If backlinks are your main goal, then think carefully about the type of content you should be creating. You need to create content that *appeals to the people that have the ability to link to your site*. Not everyone does. Most people visiting your site will be just that, visitors. To create high-quality natural backlinks, you need to find out who is already linking to content on other websites. These are the market's influencers. Find them, find what they are interested in and currently linking to, and create that content. You can then use email outreach (using tools like Ninja Outreach) to get those backlinks.

In SEO terms, links to a page are important for ranking in the search engines, so if we can get other websites to link to our pages, we benefit with better rankings. Increase links, increase traffic AND keep visitors happy with such great content.

If you are interested in getting backlinks, I suggest you check out my SEO 2017 book on Amazon. You can find links to all of my books and courses at the end of this book. Backlinks are important for all websites.

From now on, I want you to think about your content in terms of "share bait" and "link bait".

Think of visitor experience first, search engines second.

OK, so let's explore the types of content you can post on your site.

1. Articles

When most webmasters think of content, they think in terms of an article written about a specific topic. This is, of course, a valuable addition to any site as long as the article is well-written, interesting to your target visitor and gets them sharing via social channels.

Thinking of content as "articles" is probably a throwback to the earlier SEO techniques of finding high demand, low competition phrases, and writing a separate piece of content to rank for each phrase. As you know, that is not the type of content you should be creating. If you are going to write a "traditional" article, and there is no reason why you should not, you should be trying to make your article unique in terms of content and voice. Are you giving your opinions? Are you adding your own personality? Does the article offer something that is not already out there on competitor websites? Does your article stand out enough that Google will want to show it in the top 10?

For example, Julie has a website about the Paleo diet and she decides to write an article called "What is the Paleo Diet?" In her article, she wants to talk about what you can and cannot eat while on the Paleo diet.

How is she going to make her article unique in terms of content and voice? What is going to differentiate her article from the thousands of other articles on the exact same topic? What is going to make Google take her article above all of the others and put it into the top 10?

OK, I know a lot of you reading this are shouting "LINKS".

Yes, links help content to rank. However, it doesn't matter how many links you have to an article if it's not very good. Even if it ranks well initially, the search engines will catch on, and rankings will slide. The first step in getting any piece of content to rank well and STICK in the rankings is to make that content better than anything else out there, or at least making it different enough (in some interesting way) to warrant a place in the top 10.

To make her article on "What is the Paleo Diet?" different, she could write an article on the things she found most difficult about adapting to the Paleo diet. What food items SHE misses, and how she's replaced them with Paleo-friendly alternatives. In other words, she could write it from a personal standpoint and inject her own personality into the article.

An example might be that she found it very difficult to give up bread and cakes. She could then link to recipes on her site offering paleo bread and paleo cake recipes. She might also miss peanut butter (peanuts are legumes and aren't allowed), but she has a great almond butter recipe that totally makes up for it.

After writing the article, she might decide that her title of "What is the Paleo Diet?" is a little too generic and rename it something like "My favorite Paleo-friendly alternatives to old food addictions."

OK, that title is just off the top of my head, but it's a good starting point, and I can see that type of article being "share bait" in the Paleo community.

In the days of yore, webmasters would have laughed at me for suggesting a title that did not contain a keyword phrase, but you know better, don't you?

My point should be clear. Your articles need to stand out and offer visitors something that is not already in the top 10, otherwise, why would Google consider ranking your article above the current top 10? Your articles need to be interesting enough to encourage your readers to share it through social channels. It's through social sharing that other people (and search engines) will start to take notice.

A lot of the types of content we'll look at in this chapter are "articles" in the traditional sense. However, looking at them as different categories or types of article is helpful, because it can stimulate new ideas and opportunities for entertaining our visitors. Let's get on.

2. PDF

PDF stands for portable document format and is a standard way to distribute a document of some sort. I like to create at least one PDF document for a website because of its versatility.

Ways you can use a PDF include:

- Offer it as an incentive to sign up for a newsletter.
- Distribute it to a number of document-sharing sites, which not only get more eyes on the document but also offer an opportunity to get a link back to your site.
- Add affiliate links to the document and give it away. When a reader clicks through on an affiliate link and makes a purchase, you make a commission. For example, if you had a "juicing" site, you could create a PDF that reviews the top juicers, link to the juicers via affiliate links, and give the report away.
- Create a PDF eBook and sell it on your site.

PDFs can be downloaded and read on computers and mobile devices, so offer your visitors another way to digest your content.

3. Images Including Mind Maps, Infographics, Diagrams, etc.

Don't underestimate the value of quality diagrams. They can be flow charts, mind maps, or simple diagrams used to explain a point in your text. Have you heard the phrase a picture is worth a thousand words? Well, that applies to a web page too, and great images tend to be shared more than most other types of content, especially since Pinterest and other image-sharing sites arrived on the scene.

If a diagram can help you explain something, use one.

There are some great graphics packages available for creating diagrams. My personal favorite is called eDraw Max. It allows users to create a wide range of diagrams, including mind maps, infographics, flow charts, etc. You can find it here:

https://www.edrawsoft.com/

Another popular free graphics tool is the Gimp:

https://www.gimp.org/

Be warned, though, it comes with quite a learning curve.

4. Video

Google owns YouTube and probably because of that, you see a lot of YouTube videos ranking in the top 10 of Google for a wide range of search terms.

You can create a YouTube channel free of charge. If you create a video and upload it to your channel, you can embed that video into a web page on your site.

Good videos get shared a lot on social media.

Remember, Google owns YouTube and can make good videos rank highly in the SERPs.

Creating a video does not need to be expensive or complicated. You could record yourself or someone else on your Smartphone and upload the video to your YouTube channel. Alternatively, you could record your computer screen to create tutorials using freely available tools like CamStudio (https://camstudio.org/), not to be confused with Camtasia Studio which is quite expensive. Another popular free tool is Screencast-O-Matic (https://www.screencast-o-matic.com/).

Create a video, upload it to YouTube, and embed it on a page as part of a larger article.

Good videos also increase the time a visitor stays on your site. Since time on site is something that Google monitors, this can only be good for your SEO efforts.

5. FAQs

By their very name, FAQs or "frequently asked questions" are exactly the type of content you should be including on your website. After all, they are the common questions that real visitors ask.

Whenever you get an email from a visitor asking a question, create a web page on your site that displays the question and your answer. You can then send that person the web page (containing social sharing buttons).

This not only makes them aware of your site if they weren't already, but it adds valuable content to your site and keeps the person who asked the question happy. If you include their name as part of the question, they might even share the web page with their friends. Everyone wants five minutes of fame!

Over time, an FAQ section on your site will grow, offering a really valuable resource to your visitors.

6. Photos

Note that you cannot just download and use any photo you want on your website. If you find a photo that you want to use, you must check out the licensing for that photo. There are also stock photo sites where you can buy a license to use photos.

OK, with that said, how can you use photos on your site?

People don't generally like reading large blocks of text. If you can split it up with interesting photos, it makes the content easier to digest. They don't need to be professional quality photos. In fact, using your mobile phone to take the photos can add to the charm of your web pages, since a visitor can see that there is a real person behind the site.

Another excellent use for photos is as "link bait". People love funny photos, photos of animals, or babies, and just anything that makes them laugh or go "ahh".

Depending on the type of site you run, you might be able to think of photos that people would want to share. With photo sharing sites like Pinterest, Flickr, Shutterfly, and Instagram, photos can really help boost traffic (and links) to your site.

Do you want a few examples?

If you ran a juicing site, cute pictures of babies spilling juice all over themselves would be fun, though be careful not to abuse your own child if you take these photos yourself.

If you ran a pet site, the possible photo (and video) opportunities are endless, from cute puppies to the photo of your Rottweiler snuggling up to your pet rat or budgie.

If you ran a skin care website, maybe you could show photos of the "worst tan ever". Just Google it and you'll see what I mean. You could even run a competition on your site for "worst tan" photo submissions.

If you want to see how photos have been used by others, go to Google and just search for viral photos. You'll find some really great ones.

There is also nothing to stop you taking a photo and adding text to the photo, to make it funny. I'm sure you have seen these all over the internet.

7. Sounds Files

With more and more people using smartphones, sound files in various formats have become very popular. You have probably heard of audiobooks and podcasts. These are two different forms of sound files that people can download and listen to as they drive to work, go to the gym, or stroll through the countryside with their dog.

Not everyone has the time to create a regular podcast, but a series of downloadable audio files could be created in one go, and released over time, maybe as part of an autoresponder. The audio can be saved as MP3 files, which makes them instantly usable by just about every mobile device out there.

If you do have the time for a regular podcast, this is one of the very best ways to build your audience. You can submit the podcast to various podcast directories, like iTunes, and as long as you create interesting audio, you will grow an audience of people who feel a real connection to you. After all, they are listening to you in the comfort of their own home, or car, and it's a regular "meeting".

What can you talk about? Well, that depends on your niche, but I would certainly reference content on your site so that listeners will be interested enough to go and visit your website for more details.

8. How Stuff Works

I like this type of content. People are always looking for tutorials online to learn new skills. Tutorials can be text-based, with lots of screen captures, or video based. We mentioned video earlier in this chapter, so go back and check for free screen capture software where you can record your computer screen. Alternatively, you could just record tutorials, or "lessons", on your mobile phone and upload them to a site like YouTube. YouTube can host all of your video content, which is a big money-saver for you. If you want to create videos that do not appear in the YouTube search, you can create private videos. The only way to find private videos is via a link that you can share with select people.

Personally, I like a mixture of good video tutorials with a text-based version (with lots of screenshots) as well. I have found that some people prefer to watch, while others prefer to read and follow along.

9. Top 10 lists

Top 10 lists (and even top 100 lists) are always popular. They can also turn out to be link magnets, attracting links naturally from other websites, if done and promoted properly.

Look at this:

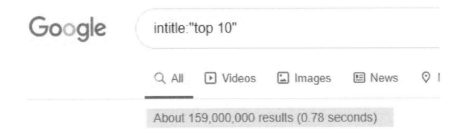

I searched Google for pages that include the phrase "top 10" in the title.

The search string consists of two parts:

1. Intitle: – this tells Google that you are interested in searching the titles of web pages for a term.
2. "top 10" – which tells Google the term it needs to search for.

We can narrow this search based on our own niche interests. For example, we could just look for the top 10 articles related to juicing:

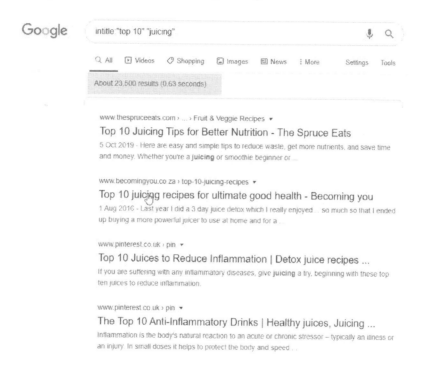

That's a great start for finding content ideas that could potentially go viral.

Try to come up with ideas for top 10 lists that will really capture your visitor's imagination.

- Top 10 reasons diets fail
- Top 10 celebrities on the Atkins diet
- Top 10 Wordpress plugins
- Top 10 reasons your car will fail this year
- Top 10 reasons to eat more spinach
- Top 10 reasons baby cry
- Top 10 things women like to hear
- Top 10 things men like to hear

Simply identify a problem and offer the top 10 causes or ways to solve that problem.

As you can see, it's easy to come up with ideas for just about any niche. Using this technique, you should get plenty of ideas.

To make it easy for visitors to share your content, include social share icons on your web pages:

Is LSI Still Important in 2018

September 27, 2017 , 1:09 pm , Blog

The two most important social networks when it comes to sharing are Twitter & Facebook.

Another site you might like to include in your social sharing buttons is StumbleUpon, but there are others, so keep your ear to the ground on what is hot.

See the social sharing button chapter in this book for more details.

10.   Resources

Resources can be anything that your visitors might find interesting.

It might be lists of articles on other websites, relevant web forums, computer software, interesting images, etc.

You could have a resource page which links out to your recommended resources, or you might decide to have a resource box at the end of an article, with a few resources relevant to that article. The idea is simply to offer your visitors more value, by highlighting resources you think they will be interested in.

If you are linking out to other websites, I do recommend you open those links in a new window so you don't lose the visitor from your own site.

11.   "Recipes"

Recipes?

Think of "recipes for a happy marriage", or "recipes for a stress-free life".

For example, if you run a "computer" site, maybe a "recipe for a virus free computer" (recommendations for anti-virus, anti-spyware, firewall etc. as a kind of recipe).

If you have a motoring website, maybe "a recipe for trouble free motoring" (check the oil, water levels, tire pressure etc. before a long trip), or even a more literal recipe for a window cleaner you make yourself from kitchen ingredients.

The point is not necessarily using the word "recipe" in the article or even thinking in terms of a traditional recipe. This is more of a trigger word to help you think of interesting things your visitors will appreciate and make their lives easier.

However, there are also recipes you use in a kitchen!

If you have any type of health site, lots of generic recipes are relevant. If you have a health site focusing on a specific problem, e.g. fat loss, diabetes, etc., you can include recipes specific to your niche (recipes to help with fat loss or sugar-free recipes for diabetics).

Recipe type content like this is great share-bait.

Writing Styles

Something you might like to think about is the style of the article you are writing.

While articles should always be informative, they can be written in a number of different styles.

The 2 main styles I usually think of are:

- Journalist/facts - where you try to be as impartial as possible, giving the information in an interesting way. Think about writing an article for a newspaper.
- Storytelling & personal - Visitors love reading real stories about, and written by, real people.

You may find that 100% of your content is a mixture of the two, which we could classify as a third style:

- A combination of facts and personal - where you provide the facts like a journalist would, but offer your own thoughts, theories, experiences, etc., into the mix.

An example of a personal storytelling style might start like this:

"Today I feel great thanks to the Atkins diet, but it wasn't always that way. Just 12 months ago, 50lbs overweight and with blood pressure running to 160/100, I had to get in shape. The Atkins diet appealed to me because I was allowed to eat lots of meat, and hunger wasn't a problem on the diet. However, before embarking on the diet, I needed to find out if it was safe" ...

This method tells the reader that you have been through their situation and can offer valuable help based on your real-life experience. They want to know how the Atkins diet worked out for you, and are more likely to trust you having read your personal story and know that you went through it.

I would limit this type of article to those topics where you have actually experienced what you are writing about. Of course, if you want to write that type of article but have not gone through the experience, you could always "interview" people who have been through it and offer their experiences in your article. This article might start off in a very similar way:

"I'm 50lbs overweight and my blood pressure is 160/100. I really need to get in shape. The Atkins diet appeals to me because I can eat lots of meat, so hunger won't be a problem like the calorie-controlled diets I have tried in the past. However, before I start the diet, I need to know it's safe." ...

This article could go on:

"Luckily I found 3 people who have been on the diet, and have had the chance to chat with them about their experiences on the diet, their results, and more importantly their blood work analysis, before and after the diet." ...

Here is another example of the personal style article:

"My sister has battled the bulge all her adult life. At 50 pounds over-weight, the final straw was when her doctor used the words 'morbidly obese'" ...

This article is based on the experiences of someone close to you, so is still very personal, and that will come through as you tell the story.

If the person was not known personally to you, but you interviewed or chatted with them to get their story (moving into journalistic style now), then the article might start off like this:

e.g. "Peter was 40 years old and 100 lb. overweight. His doctor told him that he was morbidly obese, and needed to lose weight to avoid health complications. I was lucky enough to chat with him..."

In this article, we might get a combination of the personal and journalistic styles, as you add in your own thoughts, personal experiences or advice.

Of course, if you want to keep your own thoughts and opinions out of the article, and simply report the facts, articles can become more like the pieces you would read in a newspaper.

This may be the style you prefer to use when you write about topics you don't have personal experience with, and can't find third-party stories to base your article on.

e.g. "The Atkins diet is based on high protein, low-fat meals, and has been responsible for massive weight loss in a number of prominent celebrities. However, health concerns often arise whenever the Atkins diet is reviewed....", and so on.

I don't want you to think that you have to decide on a style and stick to it. Usually, the style comes out as you write, and you should be flexible in your content writing. I **suggest you think of style more as an idea generator**. This has always helped me come up with a lot of different angles for a particular topic I want to cover.

Ask yourself:

"What personal stories can I write about weight loss?"

"If I was a newspaper journalist, what angles can I come up with to write an article that isn't the same as every other weight loss article?"

Starting with these two questions, you should be able to come up with a number of ideas, and then settle on the best one for the article. If that article ends up mixing journalist and personal approach, then so be it. As long as it entertains and informs your visitors, then you have succeeded in your mission.

Pretty much any type of article you create for your site will fit one of these two main styles, or be a mixture of the two. Go back and look at the chapter on "Types of Content", and think how each of the examples I gave could be written in a journalistic style, and in a personal style.

Examples:

- A product review can come alive if written from personal experience (which it should be). However, a certain degree of journalism will add much-needed information about the product you are reviewing. Adding in the views of other people you have spoken to will add more credibility to your review.
- A Q&A session might be mainly journalistic, but adding in your own personal thoughts and experiences can bring the Q&A to life.
- You might have a page of facts, maybe a top 10 list. That may well be just a journalistic piece, but you could add in some personal insights too.
- Think about how you would write a tutorial for something. It's mainly about writing facts in a way that helps the visitor understand how to do something, but it is also useful to add in your own experiences, tips, and tricks.

OK, it's time to start turning our attention to the "how to" write, so let's look at something I call "Niche Vocabulary" because all good text-based content has it.

Niche Vocabulary

If you had two articles in front of you, one written by an expert, the other not, you could tell them apart, right?

Google certainly seems to be able to.

How is it that Google can analyze documents and spot those that are written by experts? And remember, for the most part, it is computer code that is doing the analyzing for Google, not humans.

There are a number of tell-tale signs that a computer can easily pick up.

Think about spelling and grammar. Word processors do a reasonable job at this, so you'd expect Google to be able to as well.

Grammatical and spelling errors often appear in poorly written or rushed work. However, they can just as easily appear in articles written by experts. If an article is not proofed before it is uploaded, even the most authoritative articles could have spelling or grammatical errors.

While Google does take notice of spelling and grammar and can penalize for it, I don't think it is a major ranking factor unless it is clear that spelling mistakes were included on the page deliberately to help a page rank for misspelled search phrases.

One thing that is common to all quality articles is the "vocabulary" they use. For every topic, there are words and phrases that MUST appear in that article because those words and phrases are ESSENTIAL to that topic.

For example, if I was writing an article on diabetes, I really would have to use words like:

Diabetes, insulin, glucose, blood, type, levels, sugar and so on.

Any expert writing an article on diabetes would include these (and other essential) words NATURALLY as they wrote. This is the "vocabulary" I referred to earlier. I actually call it the "niche vocabulary", as the words and phrases will be very specific to the topic being written about.

Every article you write will have its own "niche vocabulary" that will ultimately help Google decide what the article is about and rank accordingly.

Let's take the above example of diabetes a step further.

There are different types of diabetes - type 1 diabetes and type 2 diabetes. If you had 2 articles, one on each topic and both written by an expert, would the niche vocabulary be the same?

The answer is no, but there would be some similarities.

For example, both articles would probably include those keywords we listed earlier:

Diabetes, insulin, glucose, blood, type, levels, sugar

However, each article would also include words or phrases that were a little more specific to that type of diabetes.

The type 1 diabetes article might include: autoimmune, pancreas, stops producing insulin, beta cells, genetic factor

The type 2 diabetes article might include: lifestyle, diet, insulin resistance, non-insulin dependent, adult-onset, obesity

The niche vocabulary would have some overlap, but overall, they are quite distinct.

Niche vocabulary for type 1 & type 2 diabetes

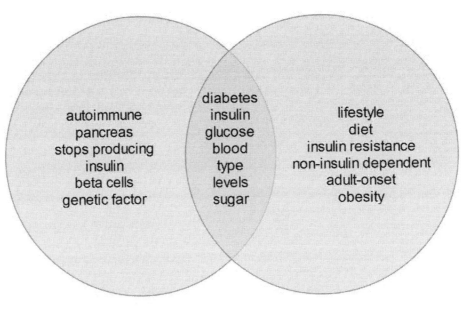

Type 1 diabetes   Type 2 diabetes

There is a type of diabetes called gestational diabetes. It is a form of type 2 diabetes. Therefore, we would expect much of its niche vocabulary to be the same as type 2 diabetes. However, there are differences, since this type of diabetes is confined to pregnant women:

With gestational diabetes included

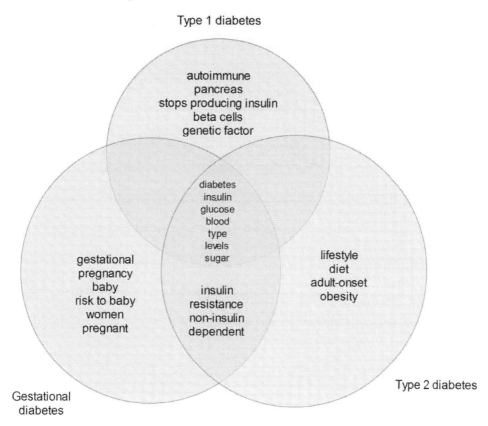

The diagram isn't entirely correct above, as some words or phrases may appear in other areas, but as an illustration, I think you can see that different topics have their own, unique vocabulary. Where similar topics overlap, you see similar niche vocabulary in those topics.

It would be IMPOSSIBLE to write a great article on gestational diabetes without using most, if not all of those words and phrases in the Gestational diabetes circle above, wouldn't it?

Every article or piece of content will have its own unique list of words and phrases that are important to that article.

From Google's point of view, looking for sets (or groups) of words and phrases on a page will help them understand what the page is about, and make it easier for them to match the pages in its index to the searcher's request. It also allows Google to find better articles on a topic because it knows that better articles will have the correct niche vocabulary.

A Quick Look at Google Search

If I go to Google and type in "Lost", Google doesn't really know what I am looking for:

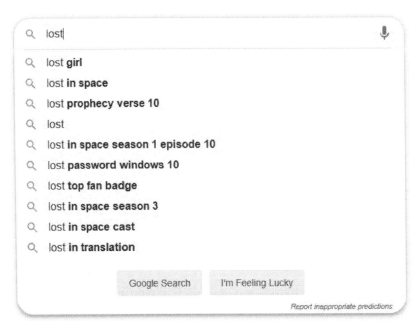

Am I searching for information on a lost girl? The Lost in Space series?

As soon as I add another word, Google can start looking for known sets of related words:

Google

```
🔍  lost freckles

🔍  lost freckles
🔍  lost freckles kate
🔍  lost freckles sawyer
🔍  freckles lost actress
🔍  freckles lost
🔍  lost cast freckles
🔍  sawyer quotes lost freckles
```

Apologies to anyone that isn't a "Lost" (as in the TV Series) fan. Google immediately associated the words "Lost" and "Freckles" and is now pretty sure what I am looking for since most of the suggestions refer to the Lost TV series. Google also knows that "Sawyer" is relevant to this search term.

Google isn't 100% sure as I might be looking for information on losing freckles!

By the way, for non-fans, Freckles is the nickname given to Evangeline Lilly's character by "Sawyer", the character played by Josh Holloway. Google knows this and offers me suggestions to help me refine my "Lost" search.

Depending on what I choose from the list of alternatives, Google will have a better idea of exactly what I am looking for, and be able to serve up the most relevant search results.

For example, if I click on "lost freckles sawyer", I am probably going to get more search results that include references to Josh and the character he plays. If, however, I choose "freckles lost actress", I'd expect to see more pages in the SERPs relating to Evangeline Lilly and her character. Think how the niche vocabulary would be different in both of those sets of articles.

Google tries to understand exactly what you want, then looks for documents in its database that have the correct niche vocabulary for that particular search term.

Incidentally, these search suggestions are based on search queries entered at Google. The ones at the top of the list are the more common suggestions, so this is another interesting way to find content ideas.

How Can We Use This Information?

It might be that you want to rank a page for "lost freckles sawyer". The old way of doing that would be to create a page, with:

- Lost-freckles-sawyer as the filename.
- Lost freckles sawyer in the title.
- Lost freckles sawyer in an H1 header.
- Lost freckles sawyer in the opening paragraph and sprinkled throughout the article.
- Lost freckles sawyer in a hyperlink somewhere.
- Lost freckles sawyer as the name of an image.
- .. and so on...

The problem is, the phrase "Lost freckles sawyer" does not make sense. Any page created as shown above would clearly be bad quality, and something Google would call "Webspam".

However, pages created like this used to rank well, and not so long ago either. This was how many webmasters created their content!

You may even still find content in Google that looks as if it was written around a keyword phrase like this, but it is becoming rarer, and Google will stamp on it when found, often de-indexing the offending site.

So, how exactly do you rank for "lost freckles sawyer" if you cannot have that exact phrase on the page?

Simple.

Find out what someone is really looking for when they type that search phrase into Google (searcher intent), and then work out the niche vocabulary. The niche vocabulary will tell Google what keywords & topic the page should rank for.

It's not as difficult as you might think.

There are pages in Google that already rank for that term.

All you need to do is study the top 10. What "niche vocabulary" are they using which is helping them rank for that phrase? What words and phrases are essential to write a good article?

Finding Theme Words & Phrases

There are a number of tools that can help you find the niche vocabulary for any topic you want to write about. Some are free, some are not. I'll show you the best free method and the best-paid tools for the job.

Free Option – Google SERPs

Simply go to Google and search for the phrase you want to rank for. Look through the top 10 results. As you read through those top 10 pages, make a note of any niche vocabulary that you see.

This can be a time-consuming process (but I will show you a free tool you can use to speed it up). This method does have the added bonus of showing you the pages that actually rank for a phrase, which in itself is a great way to spark ideas for content.

As you look through the pages:

- Note down anything that looks interesting or unique to specific web pages.
- What are the sub-headings found in the top-ranked pages?
- Are there any cool features of the content that really make the pages stand out?
- What features of these top 10 pages make them deserve to be in the top 10?

OK, I mentioned that there was a free tool to help speed up the collection of niche vocabulary. In fact, it's a web browser add-on called SEOQuake. It's available for Chrome, Firefox, Opera, and Safari:

https://www.seoquake.com/

I personally use Google Chrome, so I'll show you how to use the add-on in Chrome. It will be very similar in the other browsers.

Once installed, SEOQuake adds a button to the right of your address bar:

It should be easy to spot, as it has an "S" and a "Q" on the button. It will be disabled by default, and in fact, we don't need to enable it to use the feature I want to show you.

Do a Google search for something of interest, and visit one of the pages in the top 10. I did a search for "is cholesterol bad for you" and pulled up this page:

https://paleoleap.com/cholesterol-is-not-bad/

OK, now click on the SEOQuake button, and select "Page Info":

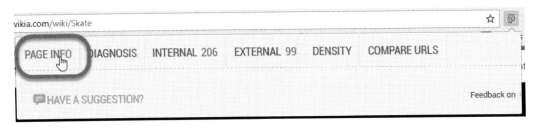

A new tab in the browser opens showing you information about the page, including "keyword density", which is pure gold for mining niche vocabulary:

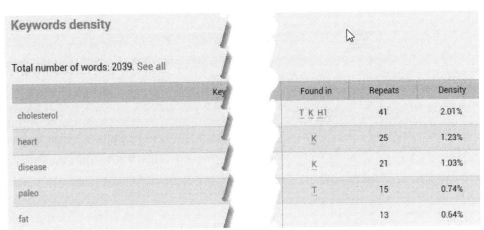

Scroll down further and you'll find 2-word phrases:

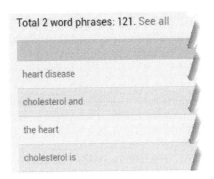

.. and 3-word phrases:

	in	Repeats	Density
Total 3 word phrases: 37. See all			
and nervous system		3	0.44%
the heart and		3	0.44%
to heart disease		3	0.44%

You may also have 4-word phrases on longer pages.

	in	Repeats	Density
Total 4 word phrases: 12. See all			
cholesterol is not bad		3	0.58%
with our top 35		2	0.39%
ecookbook with our top		2	0.39%
a higher percentage of		2	0.39%
contains a higher percentage		2	0.39%
salt contains a higher		2	0.39%
brain and nervous system		2	0.39%

The 2, 3 and 4-word phrases often have a lot more irrelevant stuff, since the tool isn't finding actual "phrases", but 2, 3 & 4-word sequences of words. However, this is still useful, it just takes a little more time to sort through the 2, 3 & 4-word phrases.

The density in the final column tells you how many times each word or phrase appeared on the page, so the more a phrase appears, the more likely it is to be important.

By looking at the information on this page, I can put together a simple niche vocabulary for an article on this topic:

Cholesterol, heart disease, fat, paleo, inflammation, food, brain, fatty acids, liver, nervous system, saturated fat, salt, bad, sodium

These theme words were all taken from a single web page. I would need to go to more of the top 10 pages and look at those as well. The words and phrases that appear on more of the top 10 pages are going to be the most important ones. Clearly, they are the words and phrases that MUST be used to write a great article on the topic. By going through the top 10 pages, you can quickly build up a niche vocabulary for any topic you want to write about.

This will then serve you as a blueprint for your own article.

Paid Option 1 – Keyword LSI Spider

I want to add a disclaimer. I created and own Keyword LSI Spider, so the following discussion is about my own tool, and obviously, if you buy, I am the one receiving your money.

This tool is a simple spider that will essentially do all of the manual work, described in the last section, for you. You simply enter a keyword phrase and click a button. The spider checks all of the top 10 web pages in Google to create a master keyword and phrase list. It then counts how many pages in the top 10 use each keyword. In a couple of minutes, you have a comprehensive list of theme words and phrase being used on the top 10 pages that rank for any keyword you choose.

If I wanted to write an article called "Is cholesterol bad for you?", I'd run that exact phrase through the spider to find the theme words that Google would be expecting to see in my article.

I ran **is cholesterol bad for you** through it and here are the results it returned.

Key Words:

cholesterol, heart, bad, disease, high, fat, blood, levels, risk, people, hdl, health, body, ldl, years, low, cause, found, diet, foods, life, liver, arteries, attack, total, lower, attacks, research, causes, healthy, women, eat, saturated, fats, types, density, lipoprotein, brain, triglycerides, diabetes, factor, food, walls, children, eggs, medical, plaque, eating, age, test, lipoproteins, cells, vascular, men.

Key Phrases:

cholesterol levels, bad cholesterol, heart disease, high cholesterol, heart attack, total cholesterol, good cholesterol, risk factor, ldl cholesterol, blood cholesterol, heart healthy, low density lipoprotein, two types, hdl cholesterol, saturated fat, blood pressure, trans fats, risk of heart disease, cholesterol lowering, cholesterol level, heart failure, artery disease, dairy products, high density lipoprotein, total cholesterol level, heart disease risk, ldl and hdl, high blood pressure, cholesterol and hdl, hdl good cholesterol, cholesterol in food, heart attack or stroke, saturated fats, triglyceride levels, hdl levels, red meat, dietary cholesterol, fatty acids, heart defects, weight loss, cholesterol numbers, major risk, risk factors, congenital heart defects, attack and stroke, high ldl cholesterol, high blood cholesterol, major risk factor, cause of heart disease, risk for heart disease, saturated fat and cholesterol, risk for high cholesterol, heart attack and stroke

That's quite a comprehensive list.

For readers that are interested in this spider, I have included a link below to a password protected page that allows you to get a discount on the full price of this software.

You can find out more details of what this tool can do, and how I use the results, here:

https://webcontentstudio.com/spider

Password: reader

Paid Option 2 - Web Content Studio

Again, I want to add a disclaimer.

I created and own Web Content Studio (WCS), so the following discussion is about my own tool, and obviously, if you buy, I am the one receiving your money. Web Content Studio takes the Keyword LSI Spider to the next level with a stack of other useful tools to help you create better content.

While I feel that WCS is the best-paid tool for web content writers, I do not want this book to be seen as a sale pitch for my own tools. I, therefore, won't go into a lot of detail here, but will instead, state the main benefits of the tool, and send you to a web page where you can see me writing an article with it.

Benefits of WCS

The main benefits of using WCS are:

1. The speed of finding niche vocabulary.
2. WCS will tell you which are the more important words and phrases (i.e. the ones that appear on most of the top 10 pages).
3. The WYSIWYG article editor and theme reports tell you how good a job you've done. When you finish your first draft, you can get WCS to analyze the content against the niche vocabulary it collected in the previous step. Any words or phrases not found in your content can be quickly spotted, as well as any word or phrase that may have been used a few too many times.

There are a lot of other features of this tool that you might find useful, but as I said, I don't want this to sound like a sales pitch. I'll leave you to investigate further if you are interested. Besides, I would highly recommend you to use the free option for harvesting niche vocabulary first.

For more details on the tool itself, visit:

https://webcontentstudio.com

OK, we know how to find the niche vocabulary for any piece of content we want to create. But before we look at the actual writing and anatomy of a good piece of web content, I bet you'd like some proof that what I am saying about niche vocabulary is real?

Proof That Top Pages Use "Niche Vocabulary"

Several years ago, when I started writing about the need to "theme" content, not everyone believed me. To help prove my point, I created a tool that could not only find niche vocabulary for any topic, but it could take that niche vocabulary, and analyze as many of the Google search results as I wanted.

My research was a few simple steps:

1. Pick a search term.
2. Find the niche vocabulary for that search term by analyzing the pages that ranked for that term.
3. Analyze pages in Google (ranking at various points, like top 10, position 100-110, position 200-210, etc.) to see what percentage of the niche vocabulary these search results were using.

If niche vocabulary was real, and Google preferred pages that contained the niche vocabulary, then I figured that ALL pages in the main Google index would contain a high percentage of the niche vocabulary. Those that didn't SHOULD be consigned to the Supplemental index as "inferior" pages that didn't offer enough value.

Let me take you through an example that we used earlier in the book – gestational diabetes. I've deliberately picked a competitive term to make sure that Google has several hundred high-quality results for this search query.

Using Web Content Studio (WCS) I found the following niche vocabulary for the term "gestational diabetes":

age, american, asian, association, baby, birth, blood, body, born, care, cause, change, check, child, common, complications, condition, control, day, develop, diabetes, diagnosis, diet, disease, doctor, eat, exercise, family, fit, food, gestation, gestational, glucose, health, help, high, hispanic, history, hormone, insulin, levels, life, log, low, medical, medication, normal, oral, overweight, patient, plan, pregnancy, pregnant, pressure, prevent, recommend, risk, sign, skin, sugar, symptoms, test, time, tips, treat, treatment, type, weeks, weight, women

The tool also found the following 2, 3 and 4-word phrases:

24 weeks, 28 weeks, 9 pounds, american diabetes association, ask you to drink, baby is born, birth weight, blood glucose, blood pressure, blood sugar level, challenge test, child health, clinical trials, control and prevention, develop gestational diabetes, develop type 2 diabetes, diabetes and pregnancy, diabetes association, diabetes mellitus, diagnosed with gestational diabetes, diet and exercise, digestive and kidney diseases, family history, gestational diabetes, getting pregnant, giving birth, glucose challenge, glucose levels, glucose tolerance test, healthy food, high blood pressure, high blood sugar, higher risk, history of diabetes, increased risk, insulin injections, insulin resistance, kidney disease, later in life, low blood sugar, meal plan, oral glucose tolerance test, patient care, polycystic ovary syndrome, pregnant women, risk factors, sugar level, test your blood sugar, three months of pregnancy, tolerance test, type 2 diabetes

That's a lot of 2, 3 and 4-word phrases, but I am not suggesting you try to incorporate all or even most of these phrases in an article. These really become useful in helping plan out the article, giving you pointers on what you should cover.

For the theme analysis, I am more interested in the single words we identified, and the words that make up the phrases.

If you look at those words and phrase, you can see how a good quality article on gestational diabetes must include a large proportion of them.

My next step in the experiment was to extract the URLs that rank for the term "gestational diabetes" from Google. What I found was a little surprising because there were only 210 URLs ranking for that term.

Could that be right?

Searching Google for gestational diabetes, I found this:

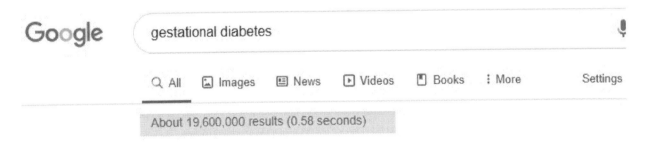

Wow, there should be over 19 million URLs ranking for this term. Shouldn't there?

Well, Google actually only ever shows a maximum of a few hundred URLs, and all the rest are pushed into the Supplemental results. If I scroll to the end of the Google results for this search, I can see this:

In order to show you the most relevant results, we have omitted some entries very similar to the 229 already displayed.
If you like, you can repeat the search with the omitted results included.

Searches related to gestational diabetes

gestational diabetes **what to eat**   gestational diabetes **test uk**

gestational diabetes **effects on baby**   gestational diabetes **in pregnancy**

gestational diabetes **symptoms**   gestational diabetes **uk**

gestational diabetes **treatment**   gestational diabetes **causes**

Previous   1 2 3

That means Google only actually rates 229 pages in response to this query.   The other 19.6 million are all in supplemental!

OK, so the next step was to import the ranking URLs into my tool, together with the niche vocabulary found using WCS.   I did remove some URLs from the list, but only because the pages reported 100 or fewer words on the web page.   I felt these were more likely ranking on the back of the site authority, rather than the quality of the content.

My first analysis was to look at those pages ranking in the following areas:

1-10, 11-20, 21-30, 31-40, 41-50, 51-60 & 61-70.

Here is the table of results the tool returned:

Position	Theme Score (%)	Theme Words Used (%)
1 - 10	100	96.8
11 - 20	99.8	99.8
21 - 30	89.5	89.5
31 - 40	93.8	93.8
41 - 50	87.1	87.1
51 - 60	100	100
61 - 70	82.7	82.7

The first column tells you where the web pages that were analyzed came from in the SERPs.

The second column is the average theme score for the pages in that group. This uses the same calculation as WCS to determine how well articles are themed, and that is important. It is based on a calculation I set up in the software to determine how well themed an article is. It is not a scientific measure. The closer to 100% the more themed an article (comparing it to the selected niche vocabulary).

The third column is the number of different theme words found in the articles from those we found initially (see earlier lists).

As you can see, all of the pages ranking in the top 70 of Google have a good percentage of the niche vocabulary. When you consider that the niche vocabulary contains 70 theme words in total, that's quite impressive.

However, what would happen if we analyzed pages further down in Google?

Let's run that experiment as well. Here we look at the pages ranking at positions 1-10 (for comparison) with those ranking at 101-110, and 191 - 200. You might expect those pages that rank much lower down in the search results (remember there are only 200 or so of them) to contain a lot less niche vocabulary?

Here are the results:

Position	Theme Score (%)	Theme Words Used (%)
1 - 10	100	96.8
101 - 110	84.4	69
191 - 200	76.4	48.1

The important column to keep your eye on is the last one. This shows the average percentage of niche vocabulary found on the web pages ranking in those position ranges.

Pages ranking in the top 10 used 96.8% of the theme words.

Pages ranking 101-110 used 69% of the theme words

Pages ranking 201-210 used 48.1% of the theme words.

It should be noted that some of the pages at the very end of the SERPs were not specifically about gestational diabetes. Not sure if Google was struggling to find new takes on the subject, so added in some general diabetes results, but I still think that last row is impressive. Over the 70 theme words found, even those ranked at the very end of Google contained around half of them.

However, this shouldn't really be a surprise since that niche vocabulary is essential to writing a good article on the topic. Any article that did not contain a good percentage has no right to be ranking in the main results. Most likely, they'll be in the Supplemental Index.

All of this goes to show that Google is actually doing a pretty good job. It also goes to show that you need to be thinking in terms of niche vocabulary if you don't want to be consigned to the Supplemental Index.

Writing content that contains theme words and phrases is a very important part of creating web pages that can rank and stick in Google. However, in the next section, we'll look at a number of other factors that you need to be thinking about.

A Side Note

Over the years I have done this experiment many times. What I have seen is that each year, for any search term, the number of results in the main index has slowly gone down to around 200 or less.

7 - 8 years ago, it was not unusual to see close to 1000 results in the main index for this term. At the end of 2017, that number had shrunk to around 370. In 2019 when I updated the book, it was 200. Today that number is 229, so very similar to last year.

Try it with any search in Google and see how many results you get in the main index.

Here are some examples:

1. Contact lenses - 180 results out of 212 million are shown in the main index.
2. Buy a motor home - 196 out of 3,280 million are shown in the main index.
3. Donald Trump - 155 out of 929 million are shown in the main index.

So, out of millions of pages available for Google to show to searcher's, only around 200 make the grade.

Is Google getting more ruthless? Or just more accurate?

Let's Write!

In the previous sections, we looked at finding the niche vocabulary for any piece of content we want to create.

Thoughts on the Actual Content

In this section, I want to take you through a "checklist" of things to consider as you write your content, and create your web page.

Checkpoint #1 - How Will Your Content Be Better?

If you've been through the manual process of collecting niche vocabulary for your content, then you will have already visited some of the top 10 pages you are competing with. How is YOUR content going to be better than those already occupying the top 10 in Google? Why should Google rank you above these other pages? What's in it for Google? We talked about this earlier in the book. You need to come up with your own unique angle for the content. Something that Google will want to show its visitors. Something that your visitors will want to share with their friends and followers. What makes your content "share bait" and/or "link bait"?

Checkpoint #2 – Title

The first thing someone will see when they land on a web page is the page title. In fact, the first thing someone is likely to see BEFORE they get to your site is the title – as that is displayed in the Google search results.

The temptation with the title is to try to include the main phrase you want to rank for, and that can still work well from an SEO point of view. However, remember two things:

1. Your title will be visible in the Google search results, so make sure it is enticing to those who are searching. Will the title arouse curiosity enough to encourage the click through to your page? Think about the last time you read a newspaper or magazine. What was it about certain articles that made you want to read them? There's a good chance it was the title. If your page is shown at the top of the Google SERPs, you are competing with 9 other pages on the exact same topic. How is your title going to encourage searchers to click to your page, rather than a competitor's page? There is no point ranking in the top 10 if no one clicks your link!

2. As we saw earlier, including the exact keyword terms we want to rank for is not important. A lot of the top ranked pages for any particular term do not include

the term in the title, or anywhere else on the page. The THEME is the important thing here, not a specific keyword phrase.

My advice is to go and see what your competitors are using for their titles and try to come up with a better one. If there are Google adverts in the SERPs, pay special attention to how they are worded (title and description). Most Google adverts will be highly optimized for the click, so is there anything you can learn there?

I'd also recommend you choose your title AFTER you have written your content because it's only then that you know the full scope of your content, and how you can sell it using the title.

Let me give you an example.

If I was writing an article on the safety of the Atkins diet, I would search Google for a relevant search phrase and see what the top 10 are using for titles. These are the titles I have to beat.

Here are the first 5 search results:

How Safe Is the Atkins Diet? - WebMD
https://www.webmd.com › Diet & Weight Management › Feature Stories ▾

Atkins Diet Plan Review: Foods, Benefits, and Risks - WebMD
https://www.webmd.com/diet/a-z/atkins-diet-what-it-is ▾

Atkins Diet: What's behind the claims? - Mayo Clinic
https://www.mayoclinic.org/healthy-lifestyle/weight-loss/in.../atkins-diet/art-20048485 ▾

Protein paradise: how safe is the Atkins diet? - NetDoctor
https://www.netdoctor.co.uk/healthy.../protein-paradise-how-safe-is-the-atkins-diet/ ▾

Is the Atkins Diet dangerous? | Daily Mail Online
https://www.dailymail.co.uk/health/article-188550/Is-Atkins-Diet-dangerous.html

If I was actually searching for this information, which of those titles stand out?

#1 and #4 use the word safe, but I'd be inclined to click on the 5th entry as that takes the idea of safety to another level, asking "Is the Atkins Diet **Dangerous**?"

However, if I was interested in the safety of the diet, how much more appealing would be a headline like:

- Atkins diet may be bad for your heart.
- Atkins diet raises bad cholesterol.
- Atkins diet linked with cardiovascular disease.

100

Now, I have no idea whether the Atkins diet is safe or not, but if I was writing an article on this topic, I would know, and I could structure my headline to make an "emotional" link with the searcher. If it is a safe diet, then headlines like these might make that connection:

- See this evidence. Atkins is safe!
- Heart disease? Not if you follow the Atkins diet properly.
- Why the Atkins Diet is safe.

A Few Ideas to Help with Titles & Headlines

- Promise to answer a question the searcher has, e.g. "Find out why...."
- Offer benefits, e.g. "Want more free time? ...." or "Save $....."
- Avoid pain, or accomplish something, e.g. "Learn how to ...... in 3 short steps", "Don't get caught by ...", "Avoid....", "Stop pain in its tracks with..", "10 ways to beat.."
- Good headlines are often personal and aimed at the reader. You can do this by talking directly to the reader and using the word "YOU".
- Appeal on the emotional level to the reader (make them feel an emotion as they read your title).
- Make them curious. E.g. "Ever wonder why....", "How do ......?", "How can they get away with...."

OK, so what about title length?

Well, I'd recommend you keep the title as concise as possible. Google tends to show the first 50-60 characters of a title, then replace the rest with ".." (see the final result in the previous screenshot for an example).

To summarize titles, create headlines that arouse interest, keep them concise and not more than 55 - 60 characters in length.

A note for Wordpress users: When you add a new post or page in Wordpress, Wordpress asks you for a title. This title will be used as the page's title tag AND the opening headline on the page. If you want to use the post title as the main headline, but something else for the title tag, you can. Install the Yoast SEO plugin. This allows you to change the title tag separately from the post title.

Checkpoint #3 - Filename

If you are using Wordpress, you probably don't give your filenames any thought, since Wordpress will automatically create the filename based on the title of the post.

In Wordpress, a post with the title "See this evidence. Atkins is safe!" would be assigned the filename "see-this-evidence-atkins-is-safe".

Now, there is nothing wrong with that filename. However, I do like to change the filename a little to make it different from the default title conversion. I would probably rename this filename to "evidence-that-atkins-is-safe". This tells Google that a human is more likely to have created the title and filename, rather than a default setting of a script. With Google's obsession for quality content, this small measure might just help with SEO, if not now, then in the future.

By default, Wordpress will use the post title in:

- The page's "title tag",
- The opening headline of the post,
- The filename.

So, if you don't change the filename (or title tag), you will end up with the same phrases in three places.

Google knows that Wordpress tries to automate things like this, and it is my opinion that automation, even on this small scale, can make your site look less professional. Where you can override this type of automation, I recommend you do, and it is easy enough to change the filename to make it a little different. Some SEOs simply remove the "stop" words from the filename (these are small words like "the", "of", etc.).

The title "evidence-that-atkins-is-safe", would become "evidence-atkins-safe".

This can concentrate the more important words in the filename, which from an SEO point of view is probably a good thing.

Checkpoint #4 – Meta Tags?

In the last checkpoint, we mentioned the "title tag". All web pages should have a "title tag". Google uses it in the search results as the hyperlinked title to the web page. Actually, Google does reserve the right to change your title in the SERPs at its own discretion, so don't be surprised if you spot that happening.

There are other tags called Meta tags that you can add to your web pages. Two of the most common ones are the Meta Description and Meta Keywords.

This is what they look like in the source code of a web page:

<title>The title of the web page</title>

```
<meta name="description" content="A description of the the web page">

<meta name="keywords" content="Keywords related to the web page">
```

The Meta description tag should be a description of the web page content. Google may or may not use this description when listing your page in the SERPs. It all depends on the search term and whether it is found in the description. If it is, then the meta description will probably be used, otherwise, a relevant string (containing the search term) from the main content will be chosen.

I would highly recommend you add the meta description to all of the important pages on your website. I'd also recommend that you make the Meta description unique. That is, the text of the Meta description is not used anywhere else on the site.

Make sure the Meta description is unique for every single page on your site. Never get lazy and use a generic description on multiple pages.

As you write the Meta description for a page, think of it as a short pre-sell paragraph, telling potential visitors why they should visit the page. If you slip in a bit of niche vocabulary even better, though do write the description for the visitor, not the search engines. Again, pay particular attention to any Google AdWords adverts in the SERPs for your target phrases. These will have short, concise, click-worthy descriptions that you can learn from. The title and description of your pages, like in the Google adverts, should complement each other.

OK, so what about the Meta Keywords tag?

A few years back, this tag was used by Google to help rank pages. If a keyword was in the Meta Keywords tag, the page had a better chance of ranking. Today, the major search engines no longer use the keyword tag to positively affect rankings. However, it is my belief that Google will use the Meta keyword tag to spot "Webspam" and penalize it. Anyone that stuffs the Meta Keyword tag with dozens of keywords is a spammer, right? You might not think so, but Google does, so don't do it. My recommendation is to ignore the Meta Keyword tag altogether and not bother with it. If you do want to use it, just include 4 or 5 unique (not synonyms) and relevant keywords, and make sure they ALL appear on the visible web page.

Checkpoint #5 - Opening Headline

We considered the page title earlier and saw how important it was to create a concise title that encouraged the click from the search engines.

The opening headline on your page needs the same kind of attention. When someone lands on your page, you want them to read the title and think "Wow, I want to read this."

If you are using Wordpress, then the chances are your opening headline will be the page/post title. That's how it's setup and that's fine. Since you created a great title, you'll have a great opening headline. This post title will also be used as the title tag of the web page. As I mentioned earlier, if you want to create web pages that have different title tags and opening headlines, you can use the Yoast SEO plugin for Wordpress to achieve this.

The opening headline on each web page should be an H1 header.

If you are building your site in HTML, then you have total control over which HTML tag is used to display the headline. You can ensure that it's an H1 header.

However, if you are using Wordpress, then the Wordpress theme you are using will determine whether that opening headline is an H1 tag, or something else. I have seen a number of Wordpress themes that inexplicably use an H2 for the opening headline. Why?

As with any other written material, the first headline should be the biggest and that is what an H1 tag is for. The H1 is also given special attention by search engines. Therefore, make sure your Wordpress theme uses the H1 for the opening headline.

It is also important that there is only ONE H1 headline on a page. After the opening H1 headline, use H2 sub-headlines and then H3s if you need a third level to sub-divide an H2 section of content.

You can use multiple H2s and even multiple H3s. However, there must only be ONE H1.

Checkpoint #6 - Theme the Content

The words and phrases you use in your content will help Google determine what your content is about, and help it make an initial judgment on quality. Important points to remember include:

1. Does your content contain the niche vocabulary relevant to the topic you are writing about?
2. When you read the content, does it read well for a human, or are there areas where you feel keywords or phrases have been inserted just for the search engines. This is usually easy to spot because the content doesn't read naturally and seems "forced".

3. Have you used niche vocabulary in the titles and headings of your content? This is something you need to be careful about since we don't want to keyword stuff the headings. If you can naturally fit in a keyword or phrase into your headline and section headers, do it, but make it natural, and write your headlines for your visitor, not the search engine. See the previous section on the title for more tips and help.

As we have said before, if you are an expert in your niche, you don't need to focus on niche vocabulary. You will automatically use it as you write about the subject you know very well.

But what if you are not an expert?

Well, in that case, you already have the niche vocabulary that you collected for your content. Check back on the chapter about niche vocabulary if you haven't completed that step yet.

Let's look at an example based on the niche vocabulary I collected earlier in the book, so we can see how to use it naturally as we write.

We looked at three different types of diabetes and how the niche vocabulary was slightly different for each one. Here are the words and phrases related to gestational diabetes:

Diabetes, insulin, glucose, blood, type, levels, sugar, diet, insulin resistance, non-insulin dependent, adult-onset, obesity, gestational, pregnancy, baby, risk to baby, risks to mother, women, pregnant

The first thing I recommend you do with your list is to make sure you understand all of the words and phrases. It's impossible to write a good piece of content if we don't understand the words we are using. It also helps to understand the vocabulary as you start planning out your piece of content. Go and find out how each phrase relates to gestational diabetes?

With a better understanding of the words and phrases, my next step is to check out the top 10 results ranking for the topic, and see what they cover. Making a note of the headlines used on these pages can help guide you in the structure of your own content. However, remember you are always on the lookout for an idea that will make your content stand out.

I went through the top 10 results for this search term and copied all of the headlines I found on these pages. Here are the H1 headers used on the top 10 pages:

- What gestational diabetes is and how to manage it
- Gestational diabetes
- Gestational Diabetes
- Gestational Diabetes
- Gestational Diabetes
- Gestational Diabetes
- What Is Gestational Diabetes?
- Women's Health Care Physicians
- Gestational Diabetes
- Diabetes and Pregnancy
- Gestational diabetes

The term Gestational Diabetes (on its own or part of a larger phrase) appeared in H1 headers on 9 of the top 10 pages ranking for that term.

There were over 90 H2 headers on these top 10 pages, with lots of the headlines being repeated across the top 10. Here are a few of the more common H2 headlines:

- What is gestational diabetes?
- Symptoms
- Causes
- Risk factors
- Complications
- Prevention
- How to Treat Gestational Diabetes
- Pregnancy
- Who is at risk for gestational diabetes?
- How is gestational diabetes diagnosed?
- What should I eat if I have gestational diabetes?
- Can gestational diabetes be prevented?
- What should I expect during my test?
- Tests & Diagnosis
- Management & Treatment
- After Your Baby is Born
- Will regular exercise help me control GD?

There were also a number of H3 headers but these sub-divide H2 headers so they are all related to those H2 headers above.

If Google is ranking these pages in the top 10, then the subject matter of these top 10 pages is what Google thinks is most relevant for the search term. Therefore, these headings give us a great starting point for structuring our own content because they tell us what we need to cover.

If we try to organize this list into a coherent structure, combining headings where possible, we might end up with something like this:

1. What is gestational diabetes?
2. Who is at risk for gestational diabetes?
3. Symptoms
4. Causes
5. Complications & Risk factors
6. How is gestational diabetes diagnosed?
7. How to Treat Gestational Diabetes
8. After your baby is born?
9. Can you Prevent Gestational Diabetes with diet and exercise?

What I have listed above is a skeleton structure for my own article, listing all of the important points I need to cover. The article would be quite long, but I like longer content (as do the search engines) and I recommend you don't split it up. Longer content has more of a "wow factor" for those that have the potential to link to your site, therefore makes better "link bait". It's also more impressive to your normal visitor who may want to look good to family and friends by sharing it.

As I was going through some of the ranking articles on this topic, one article stood out to me, because the headlines were a little different. Here they are:

- *What Is Gestational Diabetes?*

- *Who Gets Gestational Diabetes, And Why Do I Have to Be Tested?*

- *What Should I Expect During My Test?*

- *If I Have Gestational Diabetes How Will I Be Treated?*

- *Is There Anything I Should Be Afraid Of?*

- *Recommended Reading*

These headlines are talking directly to the expectant mother and use the word "I". I believe these headlines would connect on an emotional level with the visitor, who presumably wants to know how gestational diabetes would affect them, or their family or friend who is pregnant. If all of the other pages in the top 10 used impersonal and "scientific" headlines (which we referred to as a journalistic or fact-based writing style earlier in the book), then as a pregnant woman, wouldn't you like the article to speak to you as an expectant mother, rather than just get a list of facts?

This more personal approach to headlines is nice, and in this example, I think it's the first step in making the content more unique, and stand out.

OK, with the article mapped out, the next step is writing it.

This is where theme words and phrases become important, but the most important thing to remember is that you need to write naturally, for your audience. Don't obsess over keywords and phrases, as they will be used naturally IF you understand what the words mean and how they are associated with the topic.

To start, I would come up with a working title. I will almost certainly change it once the article is finished, but a working headline can keep you focused and on task.

My working headline might be something like:

Gestational Diabetes - Your questions answered

This title implies that the article talks directly to the pregnant woman, and answers her questions. It also gets the main phrase "gestational diabetes" in at the start - they are the first words Google sees!

Other headlines that would work include:

"Everything you need to know about gestational diabetes"

"Gestational diabetes - are you at risk and how will it affect you?"

"Am I at risk of gestational diabetes?"

"How will gestational diabetes affect me?"

All of these headlines contain references to "you" or "I", implying they are more personal and directed at real people. I would try to use the word "I" in each of the section headlines wherever possible, to mimic the actual questions pregnant women have during their pregnancy.

So instead of this:

"Who Is at Risk for Gestational Diabetes?"

I would use

"Am I at risk of gestational diabetes?"

Instead of:

"Screening"

I'd use:

"How will I be tested?"

When you are happy with your headlines, work your way through each headline, writing a paragraph of content for each one.

As you write each paragraph of your article, concentrate on covering the material in a natural way. Do not try to add keywords simply because you know you need to theme your content. As you work on your content, you will find that the theme words work their way in naturally.

Working with Theme Phrases

You may have found a list of 10-15 theme phrases (more than one word) during your research. DO NOT try to insert them all into your article. Typically, I'll only use 3-5 theme phrases in a long article, and those are the more important phrases that work their way in naturally. Far more important than the theme phrases are the words that make up those phrases.

For example, we identified the phrases "risk to baby" and "risks to mother". There is absolutely no need to use both of those phrases in your article. In fact, you don't need to use either of them. You will be talking about the mother, you will be talking about the baby, and you will also be talking about "risks". You might say something like:

"There are some risks associated with gestational diabetes that can affect you, the mother, and your baby."

That is fine from a theme point of view as you talk about the risks to the mother and the baby, even though you don't use the exact phrases. The fact that the words "risk", "baby" and "mother" are in the same sentence, means the words that make up the phrases are close together (proximity). The search engines look at word proximity to help determine meaning. Therefore, if there are any important word combinations (e.g. baby and risk(s)), putting them in close proximity can give the search engines a helping hand without having to try to stuff theme phrases into your content.

Someone writing specifically for the search engines might write something like this:

"Gestational diabetes can be dangerous when you are pregnant and has risks to mother and a risk to the baby."

This is grammatically incorrect and just doesn't flow very well. It's obvious the writer was trying to get the two exact phrases into the sentence, yet it really isn't necessary.

At all times, write for the visitor, not for the search engine.

When you finish your article, you should check the theme.

Checking Your Theme

First, read through your article and make sure it flows well. I recommend you read it out loud, as you will notice small issues that you'll miss by reading it in your head.

Will a human enjoy reading it?

Are there any awkward parts that need to be re-worked?

Have you used any phrases that don't fit naturally, and would be better off split into the component theme words to be re-written as a different sentence (like the risks/baby/mother example above)?

OK, now go through your niche vocabulary. Have you used all of the keywords in your article? You certainly do not have to use all of them, but make sure you have used the most important ones. For phrases, don't worry if you've only used one or two. As we mentioned above, the words that make up the phrases are generally more important. If there is a really important phrase, it's probably worked its way in naturally. If you do spot an important phrase that isn't in your article, try to get it in there naturally. If that isn't possible, just add or modify a sentence to use all of the words in that phrase, so the words are in close proximity.

You can also test your content at Google Keyword Planner to see if Google correctly recognizes your theme. Go and log in.

Click on the **Discover new keywords** box, and then select **Start with a Website** from the two tabs:

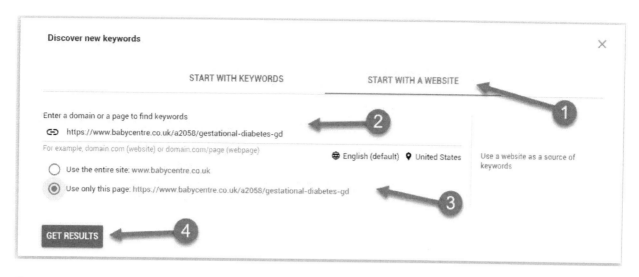

Enter the URL of the article you want to check, and select the **Use only this page** checkbox.

Click the **Get Results** button.

Check out the keyword ideas that are returned. Are they the types of keywords you would expect?

Keyword (by relevance) ↓	Avg. monthly searches	Compe
Keyword ideas		
diabetes	100K – 1M	Low
type 2 diabetes	100K – 1M	Low
diabetic diet	100K – 1M	Mediur
diabetes symptoms	100K – 1M	Mediur
diabetes test	10K – 100K	High
diabetes mellitus	10K – 100K	Low
signs of diabetes	100K – 1M	Mediur
blood sugar test	10K – 100K	High
glucose	100K – 1M	Low
type 2 diabetes symptoms	10K – 100K	Mediur

Checkpoint #7 - Above the Fold

Remember when we talked about the important Google algorithm changes? One update that occurred in January 2012 is very important to remember - the page layout algorithm, often called the "top heavy" update.

It is important to think how your web page will look like as soon as someone lands on it, and before they scroll down the page. This area of your web page is called the "above the fold" region.

The "above the fold" region is dependent on the screen resolution of the visitor. If a visitor is coming to your site with a screen resolution of 640 x 480, they might only see this:

Whereas a visitor with a screen resolution of 1024 x 768 would see this:

Juicing The Rainbow

Live, love, juice!

Introduction to Juicing ▾   What is the Best Juicer for Beginners?   Recipes ▾

Disease ▾   Nutrients ▾   In the News

What is the Best Juicer for Beginners?

Just starting out and need some advice? This article will tell you in less than a

Health Benefits of Juices v Smoothies

Juice or Smoothie? This article explores the health benefits of both.

The wonderful health benefits of juicing fresh fruit & vegetables at home

Juicing for health should be

It's difficult to know what resolution you should be testing your own pages with.

Not many desktop users have resolutions lower than 1024x768, so that should be one to test. But what about mobile users? What resolutions are they viewing your site in? I'd recommend that you install Google Analytics on your site and that will tell you the resolutions of the visitors to your site.

You should make sure your site looks good on desktop, tablet and mobile devices.

OK, so what is the deal with the "above the fold" area?

Google wants this area to contain real content. That is the stuff the visitor has come to find. What it doesn't want to find above the fold is mainly advertising, like this site:

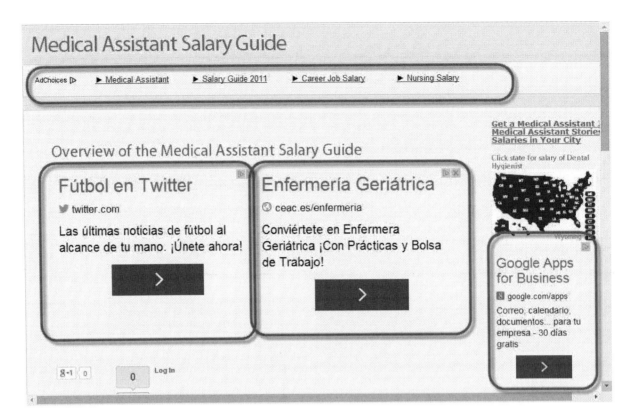

I've drawn boxes around all of the adverts.

Where is the content?

Actually, there isn't any on that page at all, but another page on the same site does have some. However, you'll only see it if you scroll to the very bottom, past multiple adverts.

Anyone landing on the page would only see adverts. This particular site was designed that way, its only purpose to get people clicking adverts. Before the Page Layout algorithm was introduced, this page probably did OK with Google AdSense. Today, that site no longer exists.

At the other end of the spectrum is this page:

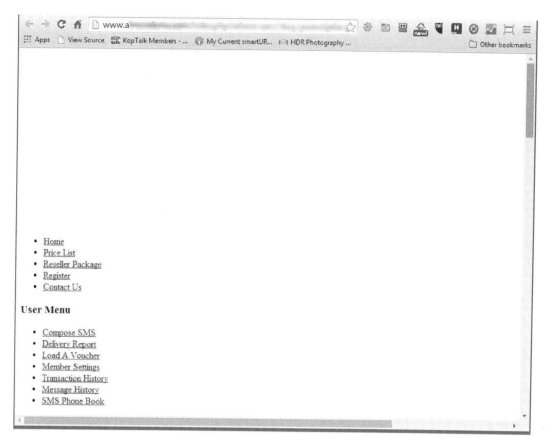

Where is the content?

This page is as bad as the previous one. There is nothing above the fold, and I doubt this was done by design. It will also suffer the consequences of Google's page layout algorithm.

What is above the fold on your pages?

Make sure it is valuable content. You can have an advert above the fold, but make sure your content is what really shines in that region.

While we are talking about the top of your web page, it is also worth considering something else.

The top of your article needs to do a lot of hard work to convince the visitor that the page is worth reading. The headline needs to grab their attention, and the opening paragraph needs to pique their interest. If you fail to make that first impression, the visitor may well just hit the back button to Google, and that "bounce" will tell Google that your page did not satisfy them. You can guess what would happen next...

Checkpoint #8 - Help the Skimmers

A lot of people visiting your site will be "skimmers". In other words, they don't want to read the whole page to find out if it is something they are interested in. They want to skim the page. If they see something that catches their attention, then they'll read it, otherwise, they'll head on back to Google.

It is always a good idea to help the skimmers by breaking up large blocks of text with "skimmables".

Definition ☺: Skimmables - stuff that helps the skimmer ascertain their interest levels.

The best way to do this is to break up your text with:

- Sub-headings (H2, H3),
- Images where they can complement the text (or even replace a paragraph),
- Bullet points. Bullet points are a skimmer's dream since they are used to highlight points in an easily skimmable format.

As you write your content, always remember the skimmers.

Tip: Use strategically placed "killer" headlines to stop skimmers dead in their tracks. Follow the headline with a few easy reading bullet points to draw them in. It's a neat trick for putting a skimmer into reading mode.

Checkpoint #9 - Grammar & Spelling

In the old days of SEO, webmasters would intentionally spell words incorrectly in the hope of ranking for misspelled search queries at Google. Those days are long gone, and it is now important to make sure your content is grammatically correct with good spelling.

Bad grammar can be an indicator of poor-quality content, and Google does look at spelling and grammar. While it is unlikely it would directly penalize content with minor mistakes, it would probably take notice of visitor feedback and could penalize pages or sites if there were complaints.

Google would almost certainly penalize a page or site if it thought the page deliberately used incorrect spelling or grammar in an attempt to increase search rankings.

Checkpoint #10 - Check the Quality

The final checkpoint is a simple quality check on all content you publish on your website.

One of the best ways to do this is to read your content aloud, either to yourself or better still to a friend.

How does it flow? Are there any sentences or paragraphs you need to re-read to make sense of them, or the odd word that trips you up?

As you read through the content, are there any words or phrases (especially those that you want to rank for in Google) that seem to be repeated too many times (keyword stuffing)?   When you read a phrase and remember having just said that exact same phrase moments earlier, you know it's being used too often.

Or, perhaps the phrase doesn't flow well within the sentence and would be better changed for a synonym. Perhaps you are aware that you only used a specific phrase because you were thinking about the search engines, and what you wanted to rank for?

Imagine giving the article to other webmasters and asking them "Can you tell what words and phrases I want to rank for in Google?" If they can, then chances are you need to re-work your content.

Always write for your visitor, not for Google.

Another thing you should think about as you check your article for quality is whether or not visitors will trust the content. I always find that visitors trust web pages more when they know who wrote them. Is there a face behind the website? An author resource box with a photograph is a great idea as it really helps build confidence in your visitors.

Another quality issue is "fluff". Essentially, it's sentences or paragraphs that really don't say anything new. Maybe they repeat a point that was made earlier, or they only seem to be there to increase word count. Nobody likes reading fluff, so strip it out of your content.

Look carefully at the "hidden" elements of the web page.   Hopefully, you won't have done any of the following. In fact, if you don't understand what I mean in these bullet points, so much the better.

Check:

- ALT tags on images. Make sure these accurately describe the image to help vision-impaired visitors. DO NOT stuff them with keywords.
- Does your HTML use comment tags? If so, are these necessary, e.g. to explain to someone else working on the site why you made changes? Or are they stuffed with keyword-rich text that will get you into trouble with Google?

- Is there any text on your page that is "hidden"? Or maybe you've got hidden links (e.g. hyperlinked a full stop/period on the page to try to pass some link juice to another page)?
- If you have hyperlinks on the page, have you stuffed the title attribute with keywords?
  e.g. <a href=https://somedomain.com title="keywords typically stuffed here">My Link</a>
  I'd recommend you don't use the title attribute when creating hyperlinks, as the title attribute has been heavily abused in the past by web spammers. If you do want to use it, use it as it was meant to be used – to explain the nature of the link so visitors see a descriptive "tooltip" when they hover their mouse over it.

As a general summarizing rule for this checkpoint:

Remove anything on your web page, visible or otherwise, that is only there for the benefit of the search engines.

Additional Considerations

The main checkpoints will keep you on the road to quality content, but I have a few other suggestions that you might like to incorporate.

Link to Authority Sites?

If you mention something in your content that you learned on another site, give that site a mention with a link (you can nofollow the link if you want to, but I tend not to if that site is a true authority on the topic) just like research papers cite other papers. The internet is meant to be a "web" of content and Google likes this type of natural link. It is exactly the type of link you hope others will give your content.

Further Reading

At the end of any piece of content, you can offer your visitors a "further reading" section. This can contain links to interesting articles, videos, infographics, etc., either on your site or on other authority sites (open external links in new windows).

A Photo of the Author & Bio Box?

Visitors love to know who wrote the content, so a photo and short author bio is a really good idea. It builds trust, and trust is vital in the online environment. If you are using Wordpress to build your site, there are themes that have author boxes built in, and plugins for those themes that don't.

Links to Related Content on Your Site

If someone reads to the end of a piece of content on your site, they probably liked it. Therefore, at the end of the content, offer them a list of related articles on your site, that you think they might also be interested in. A list of 3 or 4 "related posts" is always a good idea.

Here is an example. I wrote an article on one of my sites called "Createspace - Basic Text Formatting". This article was written for people who want to publish a book on Amazon's Createspace platform. At the end of the article, I had this related post section:

Related Posts:

1. 2. WYSIWYG – Createspace Word document to PDF
2. 5. The TOC
3. 6. Adding a new title to Createspace

These three links are all related to publishing on Createspace, so anyone that read my "Basic Text Formatting" would probably also be interested in these articles.

For Wordpress users, there are a number of plugins that can automatically create these "Related Post" sections on your pages. For non-Wordpress users, you can create these sections manually in HTML code or find a script.

Related posts sections like this, help to keep visitors on your site longer, and this is something Google takes note of.

Allow Comments

Visitors like to interact and leave feedback or ask questions. For that reason, I recommend you allow visitors to leave comments. Again, Wordpress users will find this easy to implement because comments are built into the Wordpress platform.

For non-Wordpress users, there are scripts you can use to create a comment section on your web pages. I cannot recommend any because I use Wordpress for my own websites, but searching Google for "comments script" should turn up some options.

Allow Social Sharing & Following

We are trying to create "Share Bait", so give your visitors an easy way to share your content. The next chapter shows how.

Social Sharing Buttons

If you think in terms of creating "share bait" (people like it so much that they want to share it), you need to offer your visitors an easy way to share your content. The main social networks offer buttons that you can put on your website, and if you use Wordpress, there are a number of plugins that can automate the setup of social sharing buttons.

As a starting point, I recommend you have buttons to share your content on Google+, Twitter, and Facebook. StumbleUpon is also important as it can send good content viral. If you have a lot of images on your site that you want to be shared, then Pinterest is a good button to include. However, if the images on your site are not the main focal point, I'd leave Pinterest out.

Adding Social Share Buttons to a Non-Wordpress Website

If you want an easy option, you can use a service like https://www.addtoany.com/ or https://www.sharethis.com/ which will give you the code to put onto your website. You can customize the buttons in the code that these services give you, though be aware that most services will add a button or link back to their own website. If that is not acceptable to you, you'll need to visit the individual networks and grab the HTML code for each network, in turn, to add to your site.

Adding Social Share Buttons to a Wordpress Website

If you use Wordpress, then adding the social sharing buttons to your site is as easy as installing and activating a plugin. After that, set up is usually a case of selecting which buttons you want to display and you're done.

If you have your own favorite social sharing plugin, that's fine. Use it.

There are so many to choose from.

Since social sharing plugins change a lot, I recommend that you head on over to the Wordpress plugin repository, and search for **social sharing.**

https://wordpress.org/plugins/

This will return a bunch of results.

Showing results for: **social sharing**

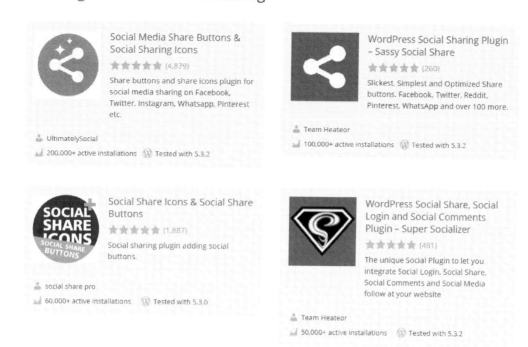

Go through these and look for plugins that:

- Cover the social media channels you want to use, e.g. Twitter, Facebook, StumbleUpon, etc.
- Have been recently updated.
- Have a good number of reviews with a high average.
- Have a high number of active installs.

Here is one I like:

To see when the plugin was last updated, click the plugin link:

Version:	1.6.2
Last updated:	3 months ago
Active installations:	80,000+
WordPress Version:	3.1 or higher
Tested up to:	5.2.5

On the right of the screen that opens, you can see when the plugin was last updated, how many active installs, and which version of WordPress it has been tested on.

Note that just because a plugin has not been tested on the very latest version of WordPress, does not mean it wont work on that version. Most will, so try a plugin if it looks a good match, even it hasn't been tested on your version.

The best way to find a social plugin that will work on your site the way you want it, is to install and activate one at a time. Go in and configure, then check what they look like on your website. If it isn't what you want, uninstall and move on to the next.

Adding "Fat" to Your Site

The term "fat" in the title of this section is used deliberately because of Google's own use of the word "thin". Essentially Google uses "thin" to refer to a page or site with very little substance and poor content.

Great content is certainly a good start, but there are other "features" you can add to a site that will:

- Encourage a visitor to share your content
- Encourage a visitor to recommend your site
- Encourage a visitor to return
- Encourage a visitor to interact with you, and/or other visitors
- Start increasing your authority in the visitor's eyes
- Tell Google that you are worth listening to

I want to go through a few ideas for you to think about. These are in no particular order.

An Autoresponder and/or Newsletter

When you first meet someone, you don't always trust them, do you? As you meet that person, again and again, trust has a chance to grow. But it will usually take several meetings. The same trust issues exist online.

Why would someone visiting your website trust you enough to buy something on your site, or something that you recommend? Of course, as you create wonderful fat websites, the trust will grow, but that can take quite some time. Autoresponders allow us to speed up the trust process.

An autoresponder is a series of pre-written emails that you can send out to people who sign up for them.

These emails can be scheduled to be sent at any interval you like. So, you could send one a day, one a week, or one a month. You could also send one a day for a week, then one a week for the next few months, and finally go to a once a month schedule.

The emails in an autoresponder can be anything you like, but the best way to use them initially is to build trust. If it takes 6 or 7 meetings to trust someone, then think of the first 6 or 7 emails as a trust-building exercise. Offer great value, and don't ask for much, if anything, in return.

Here are a few examples of how I have used autoresponders:

- To sell a piece of software. Software is created to make our lives easier, right? First off, I'd identify the various tasks that the software carried out, helping users save time. I'd then set up 5 - 6 emails, each with a tutorial on how to carry out these specific tasks the long way. I wouldn't even mention the software at that stage. After 5 or 6 emails, trust is starting to build, so I could then introduce the software and show how it can be used to automate those tasks.
- To sell a course. Similar to the first example, but the emails would contain tutorials that "whet the appetite". I would send out 5 or 6 tutorials before introducing the benefits of the course.
- To offer free courses to my visitors. I'd recommend tools in the course and use affiliate links to promote them. For example, I might have a course on creating video tutorials with Camtasia Studio, and link to Camtasia Studio with an affiliate link. Since anyone on the course needs the software, they might buy through my link, earning me a commission.

I am sure you can think of lots of examples in your own niche, but if you struggle to come up with ideas, visit your competitor sites. See if they have a signup form. Some may be for a newsletter, some may be for an autoresponder. If I find an autoresponder on a popular website, I'll sign up for it, see what they are doing, and come out with my own twist on their idea.

The autoresponder service I use is called Aweber:

https://ezseonews.aweber.com/

One of the benefits of this type of service is that not only can you set up autoresponders, but you can also offer a newsletter. A newsletter is similar, meaning you can send an email to anyone that has signed up to receive it. However, I usually differentiate between newsletters and autoresponders as follows:

- An autoresponder is pre-written and scheduled for delivery in the future.
- A newsletter is written at the moment you want to send it, and usually sent immediately, or scheduled for later in the day.

Not everyone would agree with my differentiation here, but it works well for me because it gives me an opportunity to explain how I use both - differently.

Let's take the example of a cooking website. The webmaster might set up an autoresponder with 52 free recipes. If he scheduled them to be delivered at the rate of one per week, then when someone signs up for the free recipes, they'll start receiving one per week for a year. That's right. As long as that person remains subscribed to the autoresponder, the webmaster has their attention, on a weekly basis, for a whole year!

Now, let's suppose the webmaster is running a sale on cooking pots. He could write a newsletter two days before his promotion was due to run, letting his recipe subscribers know about the forthcoming sale. When the sale started, he could send another newsletter telling his list that the sale was on.

Those that signed up for the recipes should be quite targeted since they signed up for recipes. That means the webmaster has a targeted audience he can tap into any time he wants. When the year of recipes run out for a subscriber, they stay on the list and will continue to get newsletters until they unsubscribe.

Hopefully, you can see the power in an autoresponder. To my mind, they are one of the most powerful features of any website.

A Forum

We all know what a forum is, but did you ever think of adding one to your own website? Growing a community of like-minded people, offering them a place to meet up and chat about anything is a great way to build visitor loyalty to your site.

OK, so you think it's too difficult to set up, right? Well, if you don't have a Wordpress website, it is a little complicated, though most forum software companies will help you through it.

Popular forum scripts include:

- https://www.vbulletin.com/
- https://invisioncommunity.com/
- https://www.phpbb.com/

If your site is powered by Wordpress, there is a "free" plugin called **wpForo Forum** that can add a forum to your site.

Infographics

We have already talked about the importance of images as a type of content on your site. Infographics are a unique type of image. As the name implies, they are images that convey information, and sometimes it's a lot of information.

Oxford dictionaries define an infographic as:

"A visual representation of information or data, e.g. as a chart or diagram: a good infographic is worth a thousand words."

So why are infographics a good idea?

1. They help your visitors understand your "data" in a visual and often entertaining way.
2. Good infographics often get shared, so it's a good opportunity to get new visitors to your site.
3. You can use the infographic as link bait, offering other webmasters some code that will embed the infographic into their own website, with a link back to yours.

If you want to see examples of infographics, search Google images for "infographics", and you'll see a lot of great examples.

There are a number of sites that allow you to create infographics. Two of the most popular ones are:

- https://infogr.am/
- https://piktochart.com/

A lot of these services offer you the chance to start for free, with paid options for those that need more features.

RSS Feeds

If you can (and everyone who uses Wordpress can, because it's built in), I would recommend offering your visitors an RSS feed of the important content on your website. Make it obvious to your visitor that you have an RSS feed by showing them the standard RSS "button":

So, what is an RSS feed and why bother? Well, we looked briefly at them earlier as a way of monitoring competitor websites in our niche, but let's look in a little more detail.

Essentially an RSS feed is a vehicle for delivering content in a standard format.

That definition may just have confused you, so let me give you an example.

All Wordpress websites have RSS feeds built into them, so let's use a Wordpress site for this example. Any time you create a new post and publish it to your site, the RSS feed (which essentially lists the post's title, URL, date/time published and a short description) is updated to add the new post at the top of the feed. All of the other posts in the feed drop down one place. If your feed is set up to hold 10 items, then adding a new post would cause the 10th item to scroll off the bottom of the feed and be removed as the new post gets the top spot. Therefore, the feed is always showing your most recent 10 posts.

So why bother with RSS?

Think of RSS feeds as a doorway to your site.

A lot more people stay up to date with their favorite sites using RSS feed readers. The feed reader we saw earlier, and the one I use, is https://feedly.com/ and you can sign up and use it for free. There are also feed readers available for iOS and Android mobile devices.

Savvy visitors to your site may use RSS feeds to keep up to date with their interests. By offering them your RSS feed, any time you post a new piece of content on your site, they get notified of the new content in their feed reader (which has spotted that new post in your feed).

RSS feeds ensure that your new content is pushed to users that follow your feed. That, in turn, helps build trust if they are getting new content from you on a regular basis.

A lot of people think that RSS feeds are a dying technology, especially in view of the fact that Google closed down its own "Google Reader" tool. It's argued that people don't follow feeds as much as they used to because of Twitter, Facebook and other social channels where good content is shared. However, the fact that it is built into Wordpress means you don't have to set anything up if you use Wordpress. It is already built in, so use it. Offer that feed button on your site.

Quizzes, Polls, and Surveys

People love to get involved if it is easy. They'll vote in a poll if it just means clicking a button. Surveys and quizzes can be equally fun, but maybe more difficult to get participants. However, these will add "fat" to your site, and the search engines will like the visitor interaction on your site, so don't dismiss it.

I good poll script to use on non-Wordpress sites is "Advanced Poll", and it's easy to set up, and free.

Advanced Poll: https://www.proxy2.de/scripts.php

You can find a lot of scripts to carry out polls, quizzes, and surveys at:

https://www.hotscripts.com/

Look for those with the best ratings, and try them.

For Wordpress users, "Yop Poll" is a popular choice that is updated frequently:

https://wordpress.org/plugins/yop-poll/

Software, Scripts, Calculators, etc.

You may not be a programmer, but that does not mean you cannot have software written for you. There are a number of outsourcing websites, like Upwork, which allow you to hire workers for just about anything. I personally do some programming, but that hasn't stopped me outsourcing programming jobs if I was low on time.

So, what type of program or script could be of use to your visitors?

Let me give you a few examples.

If you had a site on loans, you could offer your visitors a loan calculator that could tell them how much their repayments would be. Maybe you could offer them a mortgage calculator.

If you had a diet site, you could get a search script created that could tell your visitors how many calories a particular food item has.

Both of these examples offer value to your visitors and depending on how you designed the scripts, you could give them something that wasn't available on your competitor sites.

Other types of software include downloadable programs that can run on Windows, Mac, Mobile or other operating systems. This is probably something that is more realistic for software companies because of the cost to get complicated software created.

However, have a think about any small utility you could get created and open a project on Upwork asking for bids. You might be surprised by the quotes.

An example of a small utility might be a "times tables" generator tool for a math-related site. People could download the tool and generate times table tests for their kids. It's a fairly simple tool that would take an experienced programmer a few hours to create, so wouldn't be that expensive.

If you have software utilities that can be downloaded by your visitors, you can also submit your utilities to software websites, which in return will increase downloads and give you a link back to your website.

Of course, you may want to sell your software utility, and that is fine. You could get a trial version created which would allow your visitors to try before they buy.

Do also consider mobile apps that you can advertise on your site. While these can be expensive to get programmers to create for you, there are a growing number of sites that allow non-programmers to easily build mobile apps, like this one:

https://appsmoment.co/

You can usually start building your app for free!

Quotations & Trivia

Are there any famous quotations in your niche? Or maybe you have some strange trivia related to your content?

People love trivia. People love famous quotations. Why not include them in your content? You'd be surprised what you can find online if you look. You could use quotations or trivia at the start, middle, or end of an article.

A great place to find relevant quotations is https://www.brainyquote.com/

Just type in a word or phrase related to the piece of content you are writing and see if there is anything interesting, amusing or controversial.

To find great trivia, simply search Google for "dog trivia", or whatever topic you are writing about.

If you can find a lot of trivia on a topic, you could include a "trivia" section at the end of your article. That would certainly catch the eye of even the quickest skimmers.

For example, **did you know:**

"French Poodles did not originate in France."

"65% of pet owners have more photos of their pet than their spouse."

"70% of pet owners sign their pet's name on greeting cards."

"33% of dog owners admit to talking to their dog on the phone or leaving answer machine messages."

Would you like some more dog trivia?

Yes?

Then you get my point about using trivia on your web pages.

Video

Even if you have not recorded and produced your own video for a piece of content you are working on, there are several good video sharing sites that allow you to embed videos created by other people. The best known is obviously Google-owned YouTube.

If you can find fun or informative videos that are closely relevant to your own content, then you can embed those videos into your web page.

On YouTube, look for the **Share** link under the video, and you'll get the option of an "embed code" or just the URL (which can be pasted directly into a WordPress post).

TIP: Before embedding a video into your own website, watch the video all the way through. That sounds obvious, but you'd be surprised how many people will skip that step and just watch the first minute or two. Make sure that the video is good quality, and isn't packed with advertising to the creator's own website. Any video you embed will be a reflection on you and your own site, so only use the best.

I hope this section has given you a few more ideas for making your content "stickier" and more entertaining for your visitors.

Yoast SEO Wordpress Plugin

The Yoast SEO plugin is one of the first plugins I install on any new site I am working on. It gives webmasters a huge amount of SEO control over their website. I won't cover it all here, but before finishing this book, I wanted to show you a really cool feature.

The Yoast SEO plugin integrates into your Wordpress dashboard in a lot of ways.

If you go to add/edit a post or page, you will see the Yoast SEO plugin has inserted some options for you there:

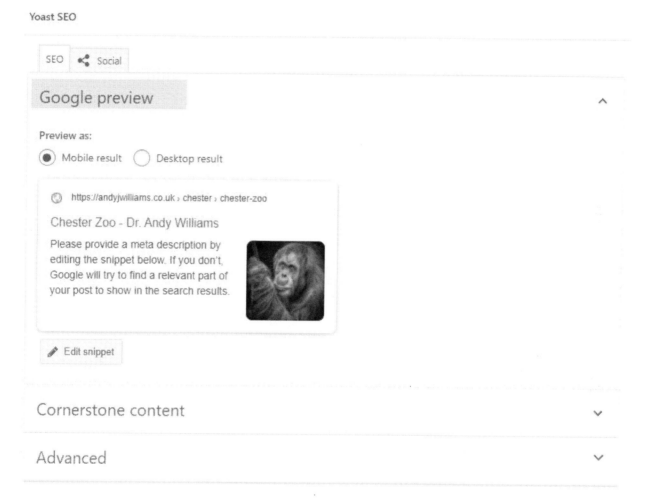

What you see here will depend to a certain extent on how you've set the plugin up, but you should all see the **Google Preview**.

Essentially, the snippet preview is intended to show you what your listing will look like in Google. You can see the URL, title, the description, and a featured image if you are using one.

The title tag is taken from the **post title**, which in turn was used as the H1 heading on the web page.

However, I can change the title tag, filename and description if I want Google to use different values.   Simply click on the **Edit Snippet** button found underneath the preview:

This allows you to edit the web page title tag, meta description AND the filename (slug) of the page if you want to, overwriting the defaults created by Wordpress.

You can see that the SEO title currently show "variables". This is how the Yoast SEO plugin constructs these elements of the page, with variables you can set yourself. However, you can also just type in what you want without using a variable.

The SEO title you type in here will be used exclusively for the title tag of the web page. That, in turn, will be used (hopefully) by Google when it lists your page in the SERPs.

When you save your post after editing the SEO title, the title tag in the HTML code will be changed to reflect what you entered. Your title tag will be different from the opening headline on your page, and your filename.

The Yoast SEO plugin is well worth investigating for the reasons I have shown here, and everything else that it can do.

Where to Go from Here?

We've covered a lot of ground in this book and you should be confident in writing great content for your website. However, many of you will want to go on and expand your knowledge of WordPress. I've therefore listed some useful resources below.

My Other Webmaster Books

All my books are available as Kindle books and paperbacks. You can view them all here:

https://ezseonews.com/my-kindle-books/

I'll leave you to explore those if you are interested. You'll find books on various aspects of being a webmaster, such as creating high-quality content, SEO, CSS etc.

My Video Courses

I have a growing number of video courses hosted on Udemy. You can view a complete list of these at my site:

https://ezseonews.com/udemy

There are courses on the same kinds of topics that my books cover, so SEO, Content Creation, WordPress, Website Analytics, etc.

Google Webmaster Guidelines

https://ezseonews.com/wmg – this is the webmaster's bible of what is acceptable and what is not in the eyes of the world's biggest search engine.

Google Analytics

https://www.google.com/analytics/ – the best free analytics program out there. When you have some free time to learn how to use Google Analytics, I recommend you add it to your site so you can track your visitors.

Did You Enjoy This Book?

If you liked this book (or even if you didn't), PLEASE add a review on the Amazon website. It provides me with valuable feedback and helps prospective students decide whether it is the right book for them.

All the best

Andy Williams

Printed in Great Britain
by Amazon

47286631R10084